Heal your inner child &

STOP IT, DO IT, DUMP THEM.

Stop procrastinating, get your life together and tell Dave to do one

VIENNA WOOD

Editing, design, typesetting and publishing by UK Book Publishing.

www.ukbookpublishing.com

ISBN: 978-1-918077-21-6

For Amy
Who encourages me to stop it
Tells me to do it
But never to dump them

For Mel
Who never stops it
Always does it
But sure as hell always dumps them

Contents

Prologue

So why, stop it, do it, dump them, I hear you ask?

Well, from my experience in my clinical work as a psychotherapist, we as human beings often get ourselves stuck in unhelpful patterns of thinking or behaving, and in most cases, we are often trying to "stop it", and stop doing something that is essentially harming us or is unhelpful to us. Or, we are trying to "do it", and implement a behaviour that is more helpful in our lives, e.g. going to the gym, applying for a new job or finally getting that huge to-do list done; or "dump them", ending a relationship or friendship that is no longer good for us, leaving a job that we can't stand, or even getting rid of some unhelpful beliefs about ourselves.

How often have you heard someone talk about somebody and say, "oh they just need to stop eating as much" or "they just need to get on with it" or "they just need to get rid of him"?

These all seem like simple, obvious suggestions. If we want to lose weight and stop comfort eating in the evenings, you'd think we would just stop it?

If we want to get up early in the mornings and be more focussed on our work during the day, you'd think we would just do it?

And if we are being treated badly by some completely emotionally unavailable piece of work who leaves us on read and is only capable of giving us breadcrumbs, we sure as hell would tell their sorry arse to jog on and never give them the time of day again…wouldn't we?

But time and time again, the answer is no, we don't.

We don't stop it.

We don't do it.

And we certainly don't dump them.

But why?

Why is it so hard for us to do something that is good for us, or stop something that is bad for us? And why the hell is it so hard for us to stop seeing someone who we know just isn't good enough for us?

The answer is usually buried deep in our subconscious somewhere, and results from beliefs built up from our childhood, which for the vast majority of the time, we are completely unaware of. As human beings, we naturally gravitate back to a feeling that is familiar to us, not because we like the feeling, but just because it's familiar. These familiar feelings and beliefs created in our childhood that we hold onto in adulthood are known as our inner child, and it is largely responsible for a lot of our current beliefs about ourselves (and just to break it to you now, the long held beliefs we hold as adults aren't always accurate!).

Throughout this book, we are going to look in more depth at what our inner child is, the types of wounded inner child, how to connect with and begin healing our wounded inner child, thus ultimately healing our adult self. You will have strategies to stop your unhealthy patterns of thinking and behaving, start doing some of the things you keep telling yourself you will do, and get rid of that person who you already know deep down isn't worth your time (you already know who I'm talking about!).

This book doesn't have to be read in order. If you want to read it cover to cover then great, but you can always skip to chapters you feel are more relevant to you.

So, sit back, get your comfy hoody on and start reading if you want to finally be able to stop it, do it or dump them. And stop accepting crumbs – you deserve more than just crumbs (and you know it!), you deserve more than the whole biscuit, you deserve the entire damn bakery.

PART ONE
THE THEORY

CHAPTER 1

The Basics – Sleep, Food and Exercise

B efore we start healing our inner child, we need to begin with the basics. Working on ourselves is kind of like building a house. We need to lay the foundations first before we begin building, otherwise the house will just fall down! It might seem trivial, but our sleep, exercise and food intake all play a huge role in how we feel. Just imagine that you really learn to connect with your inner child, face your childhood trauma, but you eat crap, don't get a lot of exercise and you only sleep for four hours a night. Realistically, you're probably still going to feel like crap! These are the most basic needs we need to meet so that we can get up and face the day ahead (let alone face our childhood trauma!). If you've already got your sleep, diet and exercise in check, feel free to skip this chapter!

Sleep

How would we ever expect to feel refreshed if we only got two hours of sleep each night? If we only needed two hours, we could spend the other 22 hours of our days being unbelievably productive, but unfortunately most of us mere mortals need an average of eight hours of sleep a night in order to feel properly refreshed (eight at a minimum, more would be lovely!).

Our sleep needs will invariably change throughout our lives. A newborn baby needs 14-17 hours' sleep over a 24-hour period. This then reduces to approximately 10-13 hours when a child is of preschool age, 9-12 hours for a school age child, 8-10 hours for teenagers and 7-9 hours for an adult (Hirshkowitz et al., 2015).

Sometimes we may have difficulty sleeping, and this can manifest itself in different ways. We might find it difficult to get to sleep and lie there for hours tossing and turning. We may wake up throughout the night, or we might wake too early in the morning and then struggle to fall asleep again. This can lead to us getting into an unhelpful cycle of worrying about sleeping, which, I'm sure you will have already guessed, makes it harder to sleep!

If you struggle with sleep, it might be worth making some changes to help improve the amount or the quality of sleep you are getting.

- First of all, it can be helpful to establish a bedtime routine – and no, bedtime routines aren't just for children! A wind down time is essential before going to bed. If we worked non-stop until 10pm, and then got straight into bed, would we fall asleep straight away? Perhaps, out of pure exhaustion! But more than likely your mind would still be racing as it hasn't had the time to slow down yet, even though your body has. Your mind needs more time to catch up with what your body is doing, so we need to prepare ourselves in advance to go to bed. Having a regular bedtime routine gives us the opportunity to wind down. This could include self-care activities such as moisturising etc, reading a book or journalling before bed.

- If you think about your sleep environment, is it conducive to a good night's sleep? Consider factors such as noise level, whether it is too hot or cold, whether it is too light or possibly too dark. Is your bed or duvet comfortable? It might sound silly, but even the smallest change to your sleep environment can really change your sleep. Do you need some blackout blinds in the summer if the sunlight is always waking you up too early? Or do you perhaps need to put on some relaxing music or sounds to drown out a busy road outside?

- It can be so common in this modern world we live in to watch TV or go on our phones, laptops or iPads in bed. We might just need to send that last email or scroll through TikTok (just for five minutes though, right?!). It is so easy to fall into these habits, but screens emit blue light which sends a signal to our brain to stay awake. When we were cavemen, there were no alarm clocks or iPhones (imagine such a thing!), so we relied on the sunlight to let us know when it was time to wake up and when it was time to go to bed. When it begins to get dark, our brain begins to produce a hormone called melatonin, which helps us to feel tired. When it starts to get light, the production of melatonin slows down, which helps us to wake up. This is why it is so difficult to get up early in the winter when it is still dark, as our brain is still producing melatonin, meaning that we still feel tired as our brain hasn't realised that it's time to get up. Equally, in the summer, it feels easier to wake up, as the sunlight starts to stream through our curtains a lot earlier (without blackout blinds of course!), which wakes us up. When we spend too much time on our screens in bed, it keeps us awake for longer as our brain doesn't yet understand that it's bedtime, even though the rest of the room might be dark. It can be helpful to have a no-screens-in-bed rule, so that your brain doesn't make the association with going to bed and looking at the light which keeps us awake.

- Other strategies for getting a good night's sleep include not drinking caffeine or alcohol a few hours before bed, as these too will keep us awake. Make sure you don't go to bed on a big meal or eat too late at night, as this can be uncomfortable to lie with whilst our body is still digesting the food. Eating something sugary before bed will increase your sugar levels, giving you a burst of energy, which isn't what we want if we want to get to sleep!

- If you have things going through your mind that you need to do the next day, it can be helpful to keep a notepad by the side of your bed so that you can write it down and tell yourself you will deal with it in the morning. Sometimes our brain needs to be appeased that we aren't going to forget about it!

- Exercise can also improve sleep for many of us. It can make us fall asleep quicker (instead of lying there tossing and turning for hours thinking about every worry we have ever had!) and improves our quality of sleep. It can be helpful to consider how close to your bedtime you exercise. When we exercise, it increases our core body temperature, which is a signal to our body to wake up (a bit like taking a hot shower in the morning!). After 30-90 minutes, our body temperature begins to fall, making us feel tired, helping us to get to sleep quicker.

- On that note, it's also important to consider the times of your showers and baths before bed. As mentioned above, when we fall asleep, our body temperature begins to drop. If we have a hot bath or shower and get straight into bed, our temperature will be elevated and will take a while to drop, meaning that it's difficult to fall asleep straight away. If, like exercising, we time our baths or showers for around 30-90 minutes before going to bed, our body temperature has time to go down, meaning it will be easier for us to get to sleep when we do go to bed.

- If you're having trouble sleeping, don't lie there worrying about it. Get up and go to another dimly lit room and do something you find relaxing, e.g. listening to relaxing music. When you feel a bit more sleepy, go back to bed and try to sleep again. What we don't want is for your brain to make the association between going to bed and lying awake and thinking!

- And finally, NO CLOCK WATCHING! Isn't it so tempting to check the clock or your phone to see what time it is, and how many hours of sleep you will have if you get to sleep now?! But is this helpful? No. Absolutely not. In fact, if it is really late and we're not asleep yet, this usually just makes us feel worse. If we don't know the time, we can't stress ourselves out over how many hours' sleep we have left, or how long we have been awake for. Ignorance is bliss in this matter!

And now for food!

We've all probably had some sort of love/hate relationship with food in our lives. I for one know that my own stress relief is chocolate – it's definitely my guilty pleasure! After visiting the dentist and needing one too many fillings, I realised that maybe I need to cut back on the sugar and find another form of stress management. My excuse to my dentist was that I don't drink or smoke, I don't even like fizzy drinks, so surely I'm allowed one nice thing! I'm not sure he agreed, but that's another story! If you think about your eating habits on a daily basis, is there anything you would change about them? If you think about your meals, snacks, fluid intake, timings of meals, do you feel as though you are eating enough of the right foods? Are you eating too much junk food? Are you eating dinner late at night and going to bed too full and unable to get comfortable? Eating might be something we do every day, but it also might not be something we give too much thought to (or maybe we can sometimes give it too much thought, which then also becomes problematic).

When it comes to food and our wellbeing, it's important to eat a balanced diet and have regular meals at regular times in order to keep us from getting hungry and to avoid any major changes in our blood sugar levels, which can leave us craving sugary snacks. When our blood sugar is low, it can lead to us feeling irritable, tired and depressed, which let's be honest, isn't fun for us (or anyone around us!). When we eat regularly, our blood sugar levels remain stable and our bodies release energy slowly.

Eating a range of fruit and vegetables can ensure that we are getting the right nutrients into our body, which I'm sure you will already know, but, it's even more important for us to actually LIKE the food we are eating. What's the point in piling our plate high with broccoli every day if we can't stand it? We might eat it, but we probably aren't going to look forward to our meals and it will just become a chore. If we find something healthy that we actually like to eat, it doesn't feel like we are forcing ourselves to eat something just because it's good for us. Sometimes there might be a way around it though – I always wished I liked bananas because of all the nutrients in them, but honestly, I cannot stand them, the smell, texture, taste…and that will never change! But juicing them in a blender with other fruits means that I can still have them but never have to taste them on their own (sorry, any banana lovers out there!).

Protein is so important and ensuring that we have a high level in our diet can help support our mental health. One study showed that out of a group of adults experiencing depression, one third of participants who ate a diet consisting of a high level of nutrient-dense foods such as protein, fish and legumes had a complete remission of symptoms (*BMC Medicine*, Vol. 15, No. 23, 2017). Proteins are made up of smaller substances called amino acids, which are used by the brain to produce neurotransmitters which help us to regulate our emotions. Dopamine and serotonin are known as the "happy hormones". Dopamine gives us a sense of pleasure and acts as a "reward centre". It has various functions in our body such as regulating our mood and controlling other areas such as memory, sleep, learning and concentration. Dopamine is made from tyrosine (an amino acid), so eating foods that are high in tyrosine can help our mental functions. Foods high in tyrosine include chicken, nuts, avocados, bananas, pumpkin seeds and dairy such as milk and cheese. Serotonin is made from another amino acid, tryptophan. Tryptophan is found in foods such as chicken, fish, eggs, milk, cheese, peanuts, pumpkin seeds and turkey. Serotonin plays a crucial role in regulating anxiety, improving mood and regulating our sleep (Bandelow & Friederich, 2017).

A lack of serotonin and dopamine can both contribute to low mood, which is why we need to maintain an adequate level of protein in our diet. Proteins also create high levels of satiety, meaning that we feel fuller for longer (so we are less likely to reach for the Galaxy bar!). It also helps to reduce sugar cravings.

Fatty acids such as omega-3 and omega-6 are essential to our brain function and have anti-inflammatory properties which help to relieve depression. Fatty acids can be found in foods such as oily fish, nuts, seeds, poultry, eggs and dairy products, and help to increase our learning, memory and overall cognition.

Let's face it, with food, if we eat crap, we'll feel like…well, crap!

Drinks

It is recommended that we drink six to eight glasses of water each day to ensure that we are adequately hydrated. Being dehydrated has been shown to have a negative effect on mental health, as our brain needs water to function (Pross & Demnitz, 2010). When we have busy lives and are constantly rushing here, there and everywhere, it can be easy to forget to drink enough. If you struggle to drink enough during the day, try having one glass of water in the morning to get off to a good start, or carry a water bottle with you. Try to avoid sugary drinks that will cause spikes in your blood sugar and are bad for your teeth! (You'll also avoid some dentist trips as well!)

What about caffeine? Although we might think that that cup of coffee or bottle of Pepsi Max will give us that bit of energy we need to make it through the afternoon, it can really have an adverse impact on our mood. Caffeine is a stimulant, a substance which can make us feel more alert, energetic and awake. This sounds great, right? What's the catch? Well, it has been found that caffeine can increase symptoms of anxiety and panic (Smith & Jones, 2020). This is due to it speeding up the messages in our brain, making us feel jittery and on edge. Also, the more we drink it, the less effect it has, meaning we need to consume more to feel a similar effect. When we stop drinking it, we may feel the need to consume more due to withdrawal symptoms. These can include headaches, tiredness and nervousness. Caffeine can be found in (but not limited to) tea, coffee, energy drinks, chocolate and Coca-Cola. If you think you need to reduce your caffeine intake, it's helpful to do this slowly, in order to avoid withdrawal symptoms as much as possible.

Alcohol

We've all been that really happy, outgoing (loud!) person in the middle of a night out. The alcohol goes to our heads and makes us feel invincible! We can talk to anyone, dance all night, and we don't care what we say or do. I once had a friend who offered to flash her boobs at a taxi driver for a free lift to the next club (the taxi driver was kind enough to give us a free lift without the need to show any body parts!) and I'm pretty sure that a long time ago in a drunken state I took a bite out of a croissant in the hot counter at a late night Co-op (oh the shame, I still owe them the £1.10). Alcohol reduces our inhibitions, makes us feel more confident, less anxious, and reduces all of our inhibitions. So what's the problem with it?

Although alcohol may initially make us feel good, it is actually a depressant, which can sometimes be hard to believe. But however good we feel during the night, it quickly wears off, and before we know it, we're crying in the kebab shop because we accidently put too much ketchup on our chips. If you notice that your mood changes when you drink a lot, it might be helpful to reflect on your drinking habits and see if there are any changes you might want to make.

How about exercise?

Physical exercise has such a positive impact on our mental health. It has so many benefits, including improving sleep, mood and confidence, releasing endorphins and reducing the risk of developing high blood pressure and other health conditions. It has been found that exercise can treat mild to moderate depression with as much effect as medication (Blumenthal et al. 2007). And it doesn't have any side effects! Win! It is also a natural anti-anxiety treatment and reduces tension and decreases stress levels.

Exercise can boost our self-esteem, as it gives us a sense of achievement after we have completed something we set ourselves to do. For example, if you set yourself a goal of going for a 15 minute walk three times a week, you are likely to feel a sense of accomplishment when you achieve this. It can also improve our self-esteem when we beat a personal record on our weekly run or if we increase the time of our walk. Furthermore, a positive body image is associated with an increased level of physical activity. The more we exercise, the more our strength, weight and shape can change, which can contribute to how we feel about the way we look. In addition, did you know that exercise can also make us smarter?! It sounds strange, but when we do any cardio related exercise, our brain is provided with more oxygen and nutrients from the increased blood flow, which then in turn improves our cognitive function (Pontifex et al., 2009). Have you ever heard someone say, "I need to go for a walk and clear my head"? Well, that is kind of what happens actually! The increased oxygen to our brain improves our ability to think more clearly. Exercise can also have a positive effect on memory and learning (Chang et al. 2019).

Exercising doesn't need to be an expensive gym membership! It can be walking to the shops rather than taking the car, it can be exercise videos on Youtube in the comfort of your own home, or doing a run around your local park. Whilst it doesn't need to be going to the gym or leaving your house, exercise can be a good way to widen your social circle if you do something that involves meeting new people, e.g. joining a class or group. If we exercise outside when the sun is shining (ok, yes that might be a push in the UK!), we can soak up some vitamin D, which has been shown to improve symptoms of depression (Lee et al. 2018).

It's important to find something you actually LIKE doing, and not something that feels like a chore. If it feels like a chore, whatever you do won't last long before you give it up. It might be helpful to think about whether there are any barriers to exercising. Do you have a busy life with a full-time job and children, and feel as though there aren't enough hours in the day? Could you do something in the evenings or at the weekend instead? Could you go for a walk in your lunch break instead of staring at the same four walls (or your phone!). Do you feel too tired to even think about exercise at the end of a long day at work? When you feel tired or stressed, it feels as though exercising will just make you feel even more exhausted. However, exercise can actually give us more energy and reduce our levels of fatigue (Puetz et al. 2008).

When it comes to exercise, it's important to remember that doing something is always better than doing nothing. Set yourself realistic goals that are achievable. Setting a goal that is too big will only leave you feeling disappointed when you don't reach it. Start off small and build it up gradually. Even if you set yourself a goal of going for a five minute walk in the first week, you might feel like it's only five minutes, but you have still achieved something! If you increase it by five minutes each week, in four weeks you'll be doing 20 minutes' exercise a week that you weren't doing before. The most important thing with exercise is to be kind to yourself. You wouldn't criticise a friend for not doing enough exercise, so why do it to yourself? You're much more likely to do something if you're compassionate with yourself and if you're positive about what you can do, rather than focussing on the negative.

Just be kind to yourself and do what you can, when you can. If your exercise routine consists of lifting cans of baked beans, then go for it!

CHAPTER 2

What is Childhood Trauma?

Now let's delve into what childhood trauma actually is. Childhood trauma refers to distressing or harmful events or experiences in our early years which have a long-term impact on our lives. These experiences can occur in various contexts, including family dysfunction, bullying, violence, abuse, or having parents who were neglectful or emotionally unavailable. The key factor is that these experiences overwhelm the child's ability to cope, leaving them emotionally affected. The American Psychological Association (APA) defines trauma as "an emotional response to a terrible event". The perception of the event is extremely important. Two children can experience the same event but respond differently based on their unique circumstances and levels of resilience.

Let's take a look at the different types of childhood trauma:

Emotional Trauma: Emotional trauma often stems from emotional neglect or abuse. This type of trauma happens when a child is subjected to ridicule, rejection, manipulation or control. For example, a child who is repeatedly told that things that they do aren't good enough, or who is frequently criticised about their appearance may grow up struggling with low self-esteem and may end up developing people-pleasing or perfectionist tendencies.

Physical Trauma: Physical trauma includes any form of physical abuse. It can be hitting, slapping, kicking, and so on. It could be a regular occurrence or a one-time incident that has led to the child becoming traumatised. If a child encounters violence at home, it creates an environment of fear and insecurity, leading to significant emotional and psychological issues later in life.

Sexual Trauma: Sexual abuse is an incredibly damaging form of trauma that can have profound effects on a child's emotional development and relationships in adulthood. Victims of sexual trauma may struggle with trust and intimacy in relationships later on in life.

Neglect: This form of emotional trauma occurs when a child's basic needs, including emotional, physical, and educational, are unmet. It can range from a parent being emotionally unavailable and not paying any interest in their child's life, to parents who are abusive or have substance abuse issues. It can also unintentionally happen when parents are busy working or have other problems in their lives, e.g. money worries, relationship issues etc. A child who is emotionally or physically neglected may struggle with anxiety and depression as an adult.

Loss and Grief: Sudden loss, such as the death of a parent or sibling, is extremely traumatic for a child and can leave them feeling abandoned and alone. Depending on the child's age and the nature of the loss, there may be a lack of understanding as to what has happened to their loved one. The impact of such loss can be all consuming and impacts the way children form relationships in adulthood. An adult who has experienced loss as a child may struggle with the fear of being abandoned and might seek a lot of reassurance from their partner. The loss of a parent can also occur through a parent leaving and no longer having contact with the child. In this situation, the child still experiences grief as their connection to that parent is broken, leaving them feeling abandoned.

Witnessing Domestic Violence: Children who witness violence between caregivers can have their sense of safety and security shattered. They may be fearful that there will also be violence towards them and may become withdrawn or resort to people-pleasing behaviours in a bid to not anger anyone. Witnessing domestic violence might lead to difficulty trusting people, and feelings of helplessness and heightened anxiety as adults. It can also lead to children growing up into angry adults who may also turn violent, as this is what they would have seen growing up.

Understanding childhood trauma can be illustrated through various scenarios:

Leah and Emotional Neglect: Leah grew up in a household where her parents were emotionally unavailable, often absorbed in their own issues. Leah had problems at school and difficulties with friends that she really wanted to speak to her parents about, but they were too busy with their own problems and told Leah that her problems weren't important, and she had "no idea about the real world". Leah's mother was highly critical of her and would always make comments about her appearance, making her feel as though she was never good enough. As a result, Leah didn't open up to anyone and felt invisible, leading her to seek attention in unhealthy ways later in life. As an adult, Leah struggles with relationships, constantly seeking validation from partners and constantly fearing abandonment. She also gravitates towards partners who are emotionally unavailable, as if she manages to win their love and approval, her younger self feels as though she has finally won her parents' love and approval, which gives her story a happier ending.

Tommy and Bullying: Tommy was relentlessly bullied throughout his time at secondary school. This experience of being socially excluded made him feel lonely and unwanted. As an adult, he finds it challenging to establish and maintain relationships and friendships due to trust issues and a fear of being judged or ridiculed again. This also leads to him becoming angry and defensive in certain situations where he feels he is being belittled.

Sarah and Domestic Violence: As a child, Sarah witnessed her father physically abuse her mother. Sarah would hide in her room and cover her ears so she couldn't hear her mother crying. The next day, everything would appear "normal" again with both parents pretending that nothing had happened. Growing up in this environment taught her that love and violence were intertwined. As an adult, Sarah might find herself in an abusive relationship or unable to form healthy partnerships because of her distorted views on intimacy.

Ella and Sudden Loss: At the age of eight, Ella lost her mother unexpectedly. She couldn't quite comprehend why her mother was there one minute and then gone the next. Her father shut down emotionally and wouldn't speak to Ella about her mother. The grief left her feeling completely abandoned, resulting in deep emotional wounds. As she grew older, Ella found herself struggling with anxiety and avoidance in relationships, fearing loss and abandonment.

James and Physical Abuse: James experienced physical abuse at home, leading to a sense of chronic fear and insecurity. James's dad believed that he had to be a "real man" and be punished for anything his dad saw as "wrong". James's mum was also scared of his dad and turned a blind eye to the abuse. This early experience manifested as anger issues in his adult life and difficulties forming close relationships, as he equates closeness with danger.

Childhood trauma doesn't just hurt as children; it changes the way we see ourselves, the world around us and influences our emotions in profound ways. Traumatised children often grow into adults who view the world as a threatening place. They are constantly on guard and hyper-vigilant to anything they perceive as a threat. This can lead to anxiety disorders in adult life. In addition, adults who experienced trauma as a child may struggle with regulating their emotions. They might experience emotional highs and lows, or find themselves feeling numb, with a constant feeling of being on a never-ending emotional rollercoaster.

Although all of this sounds scary, and let's be honest, quite depressing, the good part to this is that the wounds of childhood trauma can be healed. By connecting with our inner child, listening to the needs that weren't met at that time, feeling our feelings and accepting them, we are able to begin to heal those painful wounds. Sitting with our emotions can feel uncomfortable and painful, and it is something we all probably try to avoid, but the only way to really heal is to feel. If you are somebody who doesn't like to cry or likes to distract themselves whenever they feel something they don't want to feel, you might find this difficult. Traumatic emotions can come up when we aren't expecting them and it's natural to want them to just go away, but by pushing them down we are actually just creating more of a problem in the long term.

Nobody likes feeling anxious or uncomfortable, but anxiety is actually an evolutionary trait which helps to keep us safe. Back in our cavemen days, if we were approached by a sabre tooth tiger, we would need a hell of a lot of adrenaline to kickstart our fight/flight response to either try and fight the tiger (no thanks!) or run as fast as we could. Our fight/flight response is responsible for a lot of unpleasant physical sensations, such as a racing heart, sweating, a dry throat, limbs like jelly etc. In the modern world, we might not come across a sabre tooth tiger, but if we are wandering slowly across a road without a care in the world and a bus comes along, we need that fight/flight response to give us that kickstart of adrenaline to get our backsides to the other side of the road without getting hit! So, although anxiety and this fight/flight response is totally normal and is there to keep us safe, anxiety can also, as I'm sure we all know, trouble us when we aren't in a life or death situation. If we are in a situation which triggers a traumatic memory or upsetting emotion that we recognise from our childhood, our fight/flight response will activate all of those unpleasant physical sensations in our body and make us feel like we are back in that traumatic situation again, when in reality we are just sitting in our own front room watching EastEnders. People who have had a traumatic childhood might not have learnt the difference between normal stress levels and situations that are genuinely life threatening, meaning that they are always more hypervigilant and on guard as they perceive everything around them to be a danger. This usually leaves them feeling completely burnt out and exhausted. Sound familiar?

The impact of childhood trauma can stay with us long past our childhood and into our adult lives. Whilst the trauma might not be at the forefront of our minds every day, the fact is that our childhood shapes many of the beliefs we have about ourselves, other people, and the world around us, which in turn impacts how we see ourselves, what we believe we are capable of, how we behave in relationships, what behaviour we accept from other people and so on. Childhood trauma can have a detrimental impact on the rest of our lives, therefore healing our trauma and the wounds of our inner child, and breaking the cycle of generational trauma is essential if we want to feel happy, confident, not be a doormat for Dave to walk all over (you know who I'm talking about!), be unapologetic about who we are, and live every day as our true authentic self, and to be able to feel like at any time you can stop it, do it, or dump them. Still with me? Let's get started!

CHAPTER 3

What is the Inner Child?

Now let's get into the inner child.

First of all, what the hell is the inner child?

Well, Carl Jung, Swiss psychologist and psychiatrist, first coined the term "inner child" and said that it is a subconscious part of our personality which holds emotions, memories and beliefs from our past, and can be triggered by certain situations in our lives (Jung, 1964). Our inner child is said to be a part of our younger, child self that never leaves us. It holds the fun and spontaneous parts of ourselves that still find the excitement and joy in the little things in life, much like when we were young. It might remember the happiness and excitement of our favourite birthday party as a child with all of our friends, or that day out to the zoo with our family. But it also holds the negative memories, experiences and beliefs that were created when we were young. It might remember being frequently told off by our parents, being bullied at school, or the time someone made fun of us when we answered a question wrong in class.

When we are born, we don't have any experience or knowledge of the world. In essence, we are all sponges, absorbing everything that goes on around us, constantly taking in information from our surroundings and trying to make sense of it. We may even take in information without realising and believe that everything that happens around us is caused by us. This is due to the fact that at this age, we don't have the knowledge or understanding that other people are separate beings with their own lives, their own decisions and their own problems. For example, a child might believe that their parents separating is their fault, but as adults we know that sometimes relationships just don't work out, and that is no fault of the child.

When we experience an event as a child, positive or negative, it leaves an imprint on our minds, and forms a belief about ourselves, other people, or the world. However, due to not having any previous knowledge or experience of the world, that belief may not always be completely accurate or reasonable. These beliefs are known as core beliefs and they are held deep in our subconscious. Aaron Beck (1976) stated that our core beliefs inform how we behave and interact with the world around us. They can be positive, negative or neutral, helpful or unhelpful.

In addition, our core beliefs are responsible for creating rules that we live by, and these rules are often rigid and inflexible. For example, a person who has a core belief of "I'm not good enough" may develop a rule that they need to do everything perfectly in order to be accepted by others. Somebody who has the belief of "I'm unloveable" may try to be the perfect partner or friend so that other people react positively to these behaviours, thus making that person feel loved. However, these beliefs and rules can lead to behaviours such as people-pleasing, perfectionism and other self-sabotaging behaviours, which can often be detrimental to our self-esteem.

Core beliefs about other people could be "other people are unpredictable" or "other people will reject me". These negative core beliefs about others can lead us to become guarded and lead us to isolating ourselves, perhaps developing rules such as "if I don't open up to anybody, I can't be rejected".

Core beliefs about the world could be "the world is dangerous" or "the world is unfriendly", which can lead us to develop unhealthy rules such as avoiding any situations that put us outside of our comfort zone or that make us feel uncertain. Adhering to these rules as an adult can make our inner child feel safe and protect us from more pain, but it also prevents us from living our life to the fullest.

Our core beliefs can lead to negative automatic thoughts, which are a kind of negative self-talk that occurs in response to specific situations. As the name says, they are generally automatic and difficult to control in the moment. Negative automatic thoughts might be something like "why didn't you notice that spelling mistake in that email, you're so stupid, they're going to think you don't know what you're doing!". Our negative automatic thoughts can become our internal dialogue, telling us lies about ourselves and our abilities that we believe without question.

In adult life, our inner child often becomes neglected. As we outgrow our childhood years, we inevitably disconnect from our inner child as we navigate the increasing responsibilities that come with being an adult. However, when we ignore our inner child, it often results in unhealed wounds and unhealthy patterns that repeat themselves in our adult live. We all have that friend who we can see makes the same mistake over and over again. Maybe they end up in unhealthy relationships with similar people, or perhaps they work themselves to the bone at every job they have, and always end up burning out. They always say they won't get into a relationship like that again, and before you know it, they're playing out the same situation with another Dave, only this one has better hair and a nicer car. What we don't think about, is that we are ALL that friend in different ways. If we look hard enough at our own patterns in life, we will most likely be able to find an unhealthy cycle that undoubtedly originates from our own childhood experiences.

So what do we do then? Are we all doomed to replay the same cycles for the rest of our lives? The answer is no, not if we don't want to. The first step to changing anything in life is always awareness. How can we ever change anything if we aren't aware that something needs to change? We need to pay close attention to how we are feeling in our lives on a regular basis. Are there any reoccurring themes that you can see? Are you frequently feeling angry, sad or anxious? If so, what situations are triggering these emotions? Is there anything you are doing or avoiding in these situations that is making you feel worse? Perhaps you are a people pleaser who isn't speaking up and saying how you really feel, which is leaving you feeling frustrated and stressed because your needs aren't getting met. Maybe this is something you experienced as a child when you didn't feel as though you could speak up. Whatever you notice that your unhelpful pattern is, it doesn't mean you are stuck with it forever.

Connecting with our inner child can often provide valuable insights into our thought processes, behaviours and relationship dynamics as adults. Do you remember a time in your life (maybe more than one, but who's counting!) when you got angry and flew off the handle for something that seemed like nothing? You were absolutely livid, something inside you just snapped. You shouted at someone and said things that you really didn't mean. The next day, you reflected on this and couldn't understand why you got so mad. This is known as a spontaneous age regression and occurs when we are triggered by something that has a meaning to our younger self. We might lose control and behave like we are having a tantrum, much like a child would. Alternatively, we may cry uncontrollably, or stop talking to the person we are angry with (the good old silent treatment!). These age regressions are all defence mechanisms that might have been useful to us as a child. If as a child we had a

24

tantrum and learned that this got us what we wanted, then this is something we might revert back to as an adult. It might also be the case that we witnessed a caregiver shouting and noticed that this got them what they wanted. Conversely, we might have grown up around parents who gave each other "the silent treatment" and didn't speak to each other when a problem arose. We might not have been able to talk to our parents about how we were feeling, so not speaking at all might have been a protective mechanism. There are many reasons for spontaneous age regressions, but it is usually due to a person feeling overwhelmed in a situation and so they regress to an age and a behaviour that they felt safe and comfortable with.

In order to identify your core beliefs, you need to listen to the thoughts you have about yourself and the views you hold about other people and the world around you. There may be a theme or connection between the thoughts you have, which you may not have noticed before. Our core beliefs formed in childhood can sometimes be reinforced by our experiences later on in life, which enhances our belief that they are valid and true. If there was a particular experience in your childhood that had a negative impact on you, it's helpful to ask yourself what the meaning of that event was at the time. For example, if you had parents who didn't pay attention to you, were neglectful or abusive, you might have thought this meant that you were unloveable, and thus developed this as a core belief. As an adult, you then might notice more events or experiences that confirm your core beliefs, and discount any events that go against them. For example, you might feel low and have negative thoughts about yourself if a relationship ends, as you might then feel as though the end of that relationship means that you are unloveable, confirming your core belief. It can be helpful to uncover our core beliefs if we find ourselves stuck in a repeated pattern of behaviour that is unhelpful to us. There may be a particular behaviour that you want to change, you might desperately want to either stop it, do it or dump them, but however hard you try, you keep going back to the same behaviour. By identifying our core beliefs and the rules our younger self created in order to feel safe, we are able to reparent our inner child and meet the needs that weren't met in our childhood, enabling us to get out of unhealthy patterns we find ourselves stuck in and live a more fulfilling life.

CHAPTER 4

Inner Child Wounds

Many of us are carrying an inner child who has been wounded in some way. These wounds can manifest from various childhood experiences and can impact us long into our adult lives. They can result from traumatic experiences or difficult attachment relationships with our parents or caregivers. When we have these experiences as a child, we may act out, have tantrums, or seek attention.

As we grow into our adult years, we may not exhibit these behaviours anymore (or we might still sometimes!), but we are most likely still wounded on the inside, and these wounds can form the basis of how we interact with the people around us, our relationship dynamics, and behaviours that we accept from others. People with inner child wounds may have a low self-esteem, struggle to express their emotions and have difficulty trusting people.

John Bradshaw (1988) popularised the concept of the different childhood wounds. Many different childhood wounds have been theorised, but we are going to focus on the most prominent four:

The Abandonment Wound

If a child feels abandoned at some point in their childhood, this can form the "abandonment wound". This could arise from parental separation and one parent not seeing the child anymore, or a loved one passing away. It can also form when a child is uncared for, ignored or isn't given the emotional support and validation they needed. As an adult, the abandoned inner child may feel constantly afraid that someone might leave them. They may also feel left out in social situations, even when they are included. Adults with the abandonment wound may fear being alone and become co-dependent on others. In addition, they usually attract emotionally unavailable people, as they try to feel worthy of another person's attention and affection that they did not receive in childhood. However, the fact that the other person is emotionally unavailable means that they won't get the attention, affection or love they desire; so the childhood cycle repeats itself.

The abandonment wound results in adults becoming dependent on other people for validation, as they don't feel able to give it to themselves. They might also stay in relationships that they know deep down aren't right for them due to the fear of being alone and feeling the same wound they did in childhood.

The Trust Wound

The trust wound appears when an adult in a child's life does not protect them from danger. Those with the trust wound may have been abused as a child, had an adult betray their trust, or been lied to by their loved ones on a regular basis.

Adults with the trust wound feel afraid to be hurt and are always on guard, as they fear that their vulnerability will be taken advantage of. They usually either attract people who don't feel safe or find reasons not to trust people. The trust wound also makes it difficult for people to be vulnerable and open up in relationships, making it hard to form meaningful connections. Those living with this particular wound may also find that they reject somebody before they are rejected themselves.

Furthermore, adults with the trust wound might be afraid of taking risks due to being unable to tolerate the uncertainty that comes with risk taking. They may also find it difficult to take compliments or receive positive feedback, as they might be sceptical as to whether the compliments are true or authentic.

The Guilt Wound

The guilt wound manifests itself when a child is constantly made to feel guilty or bad for things they have supposedly done "wrong". A person with the guilt wound might have had parents who were cold, detached and shamed them for their choices if they were not in line with their parents' choices.

Adults with the guilt wound might find themselves apologising for things when they don't need to. They feel "sorry" or "bad" for things that aren't their responsibility. They did not have their needs met in childhood and become overly sensitive to other people's needs, resulting in people-pleasing behaviours. If they are unable to please others, this results in them feeling depressed and guilty, thus reinforcing the childhood guilt wound. They might stay in toxic relationships they don't want to be in as they feel too guilty to end it. If they do end that relationship, they might not be able to stop themselves from feeling bad about it, especially if they go "no contact" with the other person.

It might be difficult for people with the guilt wound to set boundaries in relationships and put themselves first. They might also attract people who "feed" the wound and end up in toxic relationships where they are easily manipulated. Equally, they might use guilt to manipulate other people, as this is something they learnt in childhood. In addition, they are usually hard workers who overwork themselves and feel too guilty to take breaks.

The Neglect Wound

Finally, there is the neglect wound. This wound is formed when a child is neglected, ignored, or made to feel unimportant. Sadly, sometimes this can be due to a parent deliberately choosing to ignore their child's needs, but sometimes this is unintentional, and can be a result of busy working parents or parents with a significant amount of stress in their life. It may also be due to a parent lacking the capacity to meet the physical and/or emotional needs of the child. Furthermore, the neglect wound could be due to a parent putting their own high expectations on the child and then punishing the child if they don't meet these expectations.

Adults with the neglect wound find it difficult to prioritise their own needs due to growing up feeling unimportant. They feel as if they do not matter, have a low self-worth and feel as though they don't deserve good things to happen to them.

A child who is neglected may repress a lot of emotions due to not getting their needs met, and this can result in explosive outbursts of anger as an adult. These angry outbursts can be due to things that seem trivial to somebody on the outside, but on the inside, the outburst is due to something that has triggered that same feeling of neglect as when they were a child. Sometimes this anger can turn into violent behaviours or self-harm.

Adults with the neglect wound may be afraid of forming connections and relationships due to the fear of their needs not being met again. They might have a constant feeling of being lonely and might avoid commitment due to their lack of coping mechanisms when things go wrong. Those carrying this wound may also find that they withdraw from certain situations and keep quiet about their problems, as this is a survival mechanism they learnt in childhood.

Identifying which childhood wound/s you can relate to can be imperative in connecting with your inner child and making changes in your adult life and relationships that will lead towards you healing yourself and your childhood wounds.

Recognising these wounds not only allows for deeper self-awareness, but enables us to begin to nurture and reparent our inner child, so that we are able to gain the sense of safety, acceptance and unconditional love that we have always been longing for.

CHAPTER 5

Love Languages and Attachment Styles

If you have heard the term "love languages" before but have no idea what they are, this chapter is for you! In a nutshell, love languages are different ways in which people receive or show love. This concept was popularised by Dr Gary Chapman (1995) in his book "The 5 Love Languages". Having an understanding of love languages can make us more aware of our needs in particular relationships, and also of what behaviours can, well, really piss us off! When we are "spoken to" in our love language, it can help us feel more connected to that person, as we feel loved and cared for. However, if we aren't spoken to in our love language, or if our love language is different to our partner's, it can often lead to misunderstandings that can be blown out of proportion!

Chapman identified five love languages:

Physical touch – connection through physical contact such as hugs, kisses, holding hands or sexual intimacy in romantic relationships.

Words of affirmation – being told things such as "I love you", "I'm proud of you", being complimented and reminded of how important you are to that person.

Acts of service – someone doing things for us such as cooking us dinner, tidying the house, cleaning the car etc.

Gift giving – giving tokens or presents, they don't have to be expensive (but can be), but thoughtful gifts to let us know that we have been thought about.

Quality time – spending time together, whether it be eating meals together, playing games, going out and doing things, or just sitting at home together and talking.

Our primary love language can often be something we lacked as a child, and this particular love language is something we will seek in our adult relationships in order to get our childhood needs met. For example, if your love language is physical touch, you may have had parents who were not physically affectionate with you. When we experience physical touch, we release a hormone called "oxytocin", also known as "the love hormone", which releases a positive surge of emotion. This hormone reduces our stress levels and makes us feel more connected to the other person. Human beings have an innate need for physical contact and having this in our early years helps to build trust and attachment in relationships. Furthermore, physical contact provides a sense of belonging and is essential in building a child's self-esteem.

If your love language is quality time, you may have had parents or siblings who did not spend quality time together, and you may have spent a lot of your time alone. This could have been due to having different interests to your siblings or having parents who were busy or emotionally unavailable.

If your love language is words of affirmation, you may have had parents who did not verbally praise you or tell you that they loved you or were proud of you on a regular basis. You may have been criticised for small mistakes or the way you looked or dressed.

If your love language is gift giving, you may have had parents who did not give you gifts; perhaps they couldn't afford to or it wasn't something that was thought of as important in your childhood. Equally, it could have been that you were given gifts that weren't thoughtful or meaningful.

If your love language is acts of service, it could be that you didn't have parents who showed their affection through doing things for you, such as helping with homework or driving you to a friend's house. You may have had to do things for yourself at a young age, or if you were an older sibling you might have had to look after your younger siblings if your parents were busy or working.

It is also important to note that this can sometimes go the opposite way, for example, if you had parents who weren't physically affectionate, you might feel uncomfortable with physical closeness as an adult and your love language might be something like gift giving instead.

People who are satisfied in their relationships often have partners who match their love language, and difficulties may occur in relationships when love languages don't match. For example, if one person's primary love language is gift giving, and the other person's is quality time, both parties may feel uncared for or unvalidated. It can be helpful as an adult to reflect and understand what our primary love language is, so that we are able to better communicate our needs in relationships. It is also important to compromise in relationships and understand that although somebody else may not use our primary love language, this doesn't mean that we aren't loved and cared for.

Attachment Styles

Now let's move on to attachment styles. Attachment styles describe the way in which a child is attached to their caregiver and the relationship between them. If we want to build healthy and meaningful relationships, it can be helpful to understand our attachment styles.

Attachment theory was pioneered by John Bowlby (1969), an American Psychiatrist, and Mary Ainsworth (1978), an American Psychologist. They both hypothesised that attachment styles as infants can lay the foundations for how we behave and respond in relationships as adults.

Secure Attachment

As babies, we depend on our parents for survival. We need to be emotionally attached to them as we are dependent on them to take care of our needs. If we had a parent who made us feel safe and secure, met our emotional and physical needs and responded when we cried, it is likely that we developed a secure attachment to them. Adults who experienced a secure attachment to their parents are likely to be more confident, more able to set boundaries, and feel safe and stable in their adult relationships. They are likely to have a higher self-worth than those who didn't experience a secure attachment, and don't become too anxious when they are apart from their partner.

However, if we had a caregiver who wasn't consistent in responding to our needs as an infant, didn't make us feel safe and secure, and didn't respond consistently when we cried, then it is likely that we developed an insecure attachment style. Infants rely on consistent reactions from caregivers so that they are able to predict how they will react in the future. By responding inconsistently, infants are unable to predict their ceregiver's behaviours and end up feeling confused and insecure. There are said to be three insecure attachment styles:

Anxious Avoidant Attachment

Anxious avoidant attachment develops when a caregiver responds inconsistently to their child's needs. They may have responded appropriately and met their child's emotional and physical needs some of the time, but at other times they would be distracted or emotionally unavailable. This behaviour leaves a child unsure about whether their needs will be met and anxious about how their caregiver will respond to them. Adults who had an anxious avoidant attachment are usually anxious about their relationships and may be clingy and always feel the need to be shown love and attention. They may find it difficult to adhere to boundaries and might feel anxious when they are away from their partner, which can sometimes result in jealousy or controlling behaviour in order to keep their partner close to them. They might need constant reassurance from their partner and may find it difficult to maintain relationships.

Avoidant (Dismissive) Attachment

Avoidant (dismissive) attachment develops when a caregiver rarely meets their child's needs and the child needs to emotionally distance themselves from them in order to protect themselves. Children in this category are more likely to self-soothe as they know that their caregiver is not going to meet their needs. Adults with this attachment style don't like relying on other people and are cautious about forming close emotional connections. They tend to be independent and feel uncomfortable in close relationships and may withdraw when people get close. They are likely to prefer shorter, more casual relationships than long term serious ones and are likely to emotionally distance themselves from their partner.

Disorganised Attachment

Disorganised attachment develops when a child feels fearful of their parent as a result of trauma, neglect or abuse. The parent might have comforted their child at times, but this would have been inconsistent due to the parent's erratic and emotionally or physically abusive behaviour. This leaves the child feeling confused about relationships and this type of trauma has a lasting impact on their relationships later on in life. Adults with a disorganised attachment style don't usually feel safe in relationships and will usually repeat the patterns of abuse in their adult relationships. They might be jealous and controlling, which can lead to angry outbursts and abusive behaviour. Deep down, they might long for a close and safe relationship, but are scared of being rejected and hurt again.

If you feel that you relate to one of the insecure attachment styles, don't worry, you're not doomed for life! There are things you can do to help move towards a more secure attachment. It can be helpful to work on your self-esteem, be compassionate with yourself and set healthy boundaries in relationships (you can skip ahead to those particular chapters if you like!).

It is helpful to be aware of both your love languages and your attachment style, as these can have a profound effect on your adult relationships and how you deal with obstacles, especially when there is a threat to the relationship or friendship. If you have a secure attachment style, you will feel more able to communicate your thoughts and emotions when there is a problem in the relationship, whereas you may become clingy, possessive or withdrawn if you identify more with the insecure attachment styles. By being aware of your attachment style and how this impacts your behaviour and communication, this will help you to be able to identify problems in your relationship or friendship and overcome them without triggering your inner child (and throwing all your toys out of the pram!).

CHAPTER 6

Connecting with your Inner Child

As we go through this book, we will be talking about connecting with your inner child in order to heal your childhood trauma. There are different ways to connect with your inner child and there may be some that you feel work, and some that don't, and that's absolutely fine! One size doesn't fit all, you need to find out what works for you!

You might be wondering why we want to connect with our inner child in the first place. I can already hear you asking, why is this important? What good will it do?

Well, connecting with our inner child allows us to begin acknowledging that this part of us exists. By connecting with our younger self, we can identify and heal unresolved issues and traumas that still affect our emotions and behaviours in adulthood. If you find yourself becoming extremely emotional in particular situations, it's likely that that emotion comes from a younger you, and we need to be able to connect with the younger part of ourselves to find out exactly what is going on and why they are feeling the way they are. For example, if you feel utterly devastated and rejected every time a relationship ends, it might be helpful to look back at your childhood at a time when you felt abandoned and ask your younger self how you were feeling and what you needed at that time. Being able to connect with our inner child in this way allows us to give her the reassurance and unconditional love she never had as a child and ultimately reparent ourselves. Reparenting is the process of providing ourselves with the nurturing, love, validation, and support that may have been missing or inadequate during our childhood. It involves consciously addressing and healing past emotional wounds by acting in a caring, compassionate way towards our inner child. As the title says, it involves speaking to yourself in the way you would speak to your child if you are a parent. It's kind of like becoming the parent you never had, but to yourself.

Engaging with this part of ourselves enables us to better understand our emotional responses and learn to express them more healthily instead of losing our shit over something that really isn't that bad! (I'm sure we have all been there once or twice!) The inner child often reflects unmet needs from our childhood and by recognising these needs, we can take steps to fulfil them in our adult lives.

Finally, many negative patterns of behaviour stem from unresolved childhood issues. By connecting with our inner child, we can learn more constructive coping strategies and break free from dysfunctional and unhealthy patterns in our lives.

Let's take a look at some ways to connect with your inner child:

Write a letter to your inner child: Writing a letter might seem a bit old-fashioned (I mean who even uses a pen and paper anymore!), but it's one of the best ways to have an open dialogue with our younger self. The key here is to give your inner child the most heartfelt letter possible. Begin with "Dear little me," and let the words flow onto the page. Don't worry about what you will say or whether you think what you have written sounds stupid, it's for your eyes only. This is a chance for you to speak to your inner child with kindness and to reassure them that they are loved no matter what. Take this opportunity to acknowledge their unmet wants and needs, and to ask them what they need at this moment. Tell them that you are here now, and that you will always be here for them. This method usually makes people feel emotional, so make sure you are somewhere you feel comfortable and won't be disturbed. You may want to focus the letter on a particular time or situation in your childhood and tell your younger self everything you needed to hear at the time.

Speak to a photo of your younger self: Dig through that old photo album (or your iPhone depending on when you were born!) and look at a picture of yourself when you were a child. This is your time to sit down with it and talk to your younger self in the photo. I know this sounds a bit mad but hear me out!

First of all, place the photo in front of you and try to imagine yourself at that moment in time. Try and remember how you were feeling at that time and what was going on in your life. Listen to what your younger self says to you. You're likely to feel a rush of emotions, whether it's hurt, pain, joy, or sadness. That's completely normal. Just make sure to validate those feelings and show your younger self that you are loved. Like the letter method, this can feel quite emotional so make sure you have time to do this where you won't be disturbed. Again, you might want to focus this exercise on a particular time in your childhood that you found difficult. For example, if you were bullied at school, you might want to tell your younger self that this wasn't your fault and it didn't mean that you aren't good enough/worthy or whatever your interpretation was at the time. Let your child self know that they are loved just the way they are.

Mindfulness and meditation: Connecting with your inner child through mindfulness and meditation is a powerful approach that enables us to tap into our subconscious thoughts and feelings. You can use guided meditations that specifically focus on connecting with your inner child. Alternatively, you can work through an inner child visualisation. Find a quiet place, close your eyes, and take a few deep breaths. Imagine yourself walking through a sunny field. Visualise a younger version of yourself running towards you with arms wide open. When they reach you, embrace them. This is your time to engage in a conversation with them. Ask them how they are feeling, what their life is like, whether there is anything they are struggling with. This is your time to reassure them and tell them that you are there for them and that you will always love them no matter what. You can also use the bedroom method for this. Sit down, close your eyes and take a few deep breaths. Imagine your childhood bedroom with your younger self sitting on the bed. Sit down next to them. Ask them how they are feeling, or if anything is bothering them. This is another opportunity for you to have an open and honest talk with your younger self.

Journalling: Setting some time aside to journal can really help you connect with your inner child on a deeper level. Firstly, find a safe space and time to sit down and write where you won't be disturbed. Think about your intention before you begin writing. What I mean by this is, ask yourself what you want to get out of this journalling session. Although the ultimate goal is to connect with your inner child, there could be different reasons for this. For example, do you want to explore your inner child's unmet needs and emotions at a particular time in your life that is mirroring a current situation, or do you want to get in touch with the fun and creative part of your inner child? Setting an intention for your journal entry will help prompt some questions you can ask your inner child so you can get the best out of your journalling session.

If you are trying to connect with your inner child to explore their unmet needs and emotions at a difficult time in your life, you might want to ask questions such as:

- How did you feel during this difficult time?
- What did you want or need at that moment?
- What do you wish could have happened differently?
- Who did you feel safe with? Who did you feel unsafe with?
- What worried or scared you the most during that time?
- Were there any good memories in this difficult time?
- How did you cope with the pain back then?
- What does your inner child need to hear right now?

If, on the other hand, the purpose of your journal entry is to get in touch with the fun and creative part of your inner child, you might want to ask questions such as:

- What was your favourite thing to do for fun as a child?
- What was your favourite game as a child? Why did you love it so much?
- What were your favourite stories or characters when you were a child?
- What did you like about your favourite story, and what personality traits did you like about your favourite character?
- What made you laugh the most when you were younger?
- Where did you like to have fun when you were a child? (for example, the park, a beach, your bedroom)
- What are the moments where you felt most free? How can you re-create these moments now?
- Imagine a day in the life of your inner child. What adventures do you go on together?

- What would you do if you had an entire day to yourself with no responsibilities?
- What would you tell your adult self about how to have more fun?

Try writing freely without judgement. Your inner child might surprise you!

Play: Another way to connect with your inner child is through play. Think about it, how much time do we spend playing as an adult? Probably not a lot! Think about what you enjoyed doing as a child? When was the last time you played tag or built a fort with cushions? It doesn't just make you feel young again, but it can really help us connect with our inner child on a deeper level. Here are some ideas for connecting with your inner child through play:

- Bring out the board games – does anyone remember "Guess Who"?!
- Try painting or colouring in a colouring book. Yes, that's right! Crayons are not just for kids!
- Dance around your living room to your favourite childhood songs.
- Have you got any old video games or old game consoles hidden away in a box in the loft? I used to have a Sega Megadrive (if you were born around the early 90s you might remember this!) but once in a while when I dig it out and play Alex the Kid (does anyone else remember this or is it just me?!) I'm immediately taken back to my younger years.
- Read a book or watch a film from your childhood (Hocus Pocus anyone?!)

As you engage in these activities, try and remember to be present and focus on the sensations, feelings and joys of the moment. Let go of adult concerns and allow yourself to put aside responsibilities and adult worries whilst you play. And remember, engaging in play to connect with your inner child is not about being the best or winning, it's about having fun!

Go for a walk in nature: Nature has a magical way of helping us reconnect with ourselves. It often encourages a sense of wonder and curiosity, similar to how we viewed the world as children. Observing the colours of the leaves, the sound of rustling trees or watching the movement of animals can evoke feelings of joy and fascination much like when we were a child. It also allows for play, as you might find yourself skipping over stones or climbing over fallen logs. To make the most of your walk, try to be completely present and really immerse yourself in your surroundings. Leave your phone behind (or just keep it in your bag so you have it for safety reasons!) and make sure you're completely present in the moment, paying attention to what is around you rather than scrolling on your phone.

Go for a drive: Take your inner child for a drive! This sounds weird I know, but visualise your inner child sitting in the passenger seat and imagine you are able to talk to them. Talk to them and ask how they are feeling and whether there is anything they want to talk to you about. Sometimes going for a drive can give us time to think and reflect without anything else to distract us, so you can use this opportunity to really connect with your inner child. If you're stuck in a traffic jam you can use this time to help with your inner child healing rather than getting stressed about something you have no control over!

Spend time with children: Spending time with children is a quick and easy way to quickly connect with your inner child. Children have an innate ability to play and find happiness in simple activities. By joining in their games, whether it's hide and seek, building blocks or doing arts and crafts, you can rediscover the fun and creative side of you that might have diminished in adulthood. After all, in our adult lives we're all too busy trying to get things done that we often forget to just stop and be in the moment. So next time your child asks you to play, forget about that huge pile of washing you've got to do for now and throw yourself into being fully present in whatever it is they are wanting you to play.

As we have seen, there are SO many ways to connect with your inner child, depending on what the reason for connecting is. Engaging with our younger self allows us to revisit and process past experiences, emotions and traumas in a way that isn't possible without that connection. When we learn to connect with this part of ourselves, it helps us to live more authentically and align our life with our core values and desires and break out of unhealthy cycles that are holding us back in life.

CHAPTER 7
The Shadow Self

I magine going into the office on a Monday morning wearing a bright yellow post-it note stuck to your forehead with all of the parts of yourself that you dislike and try to repress. How would you feel going to meetings, speaking to your boss, or even making a cup of coffee with your work colleagues whilst having this on display all the time? I'm guessing not great! Well, this notion is known as the shadow self, the part of us that tells us we are bad in some way or another.

The term "shadow self" was first coined by psychoanalyst Carl Jung (1964). It has been suggested that we all have a shadow self (it's not as dark and scary as it sounds!) which consists of the traits in ourselves that we see as unacceptable or undesirable. These may include certain emotions or feelings such as anger, envy, or insecurity that society or our upbringing taught us to suppress. If you grew up in an environment where you weren't allowed to express your emotions, especially negative ones, you might have grown up with a belief that certain emotions are bad, or maybe you believe that if you feel angry about something that means you're a bad person, leading you to supress your emotions as an adult.

As well as emotions, our shadow self also consists of traits or characteristics that we dislike, such as selfishness or aggression, and certain desires - longings or impulses that conflict with how we see ourselves or the norms that society imposes on us.

Often, we learn to suppress these parts of ourselves during our childhood, either as a survival strategy or as a means of conforming to our parents' or society's views. For example, someone who prides themselves on being calm and collected might have a shadow self that holds repressed anger. This repressed anger can manifest in passive aggressive behaviour or sudden outbursts in stressful situations.

Jung suggested that by acknowledging and integrating our shadow self, we can achieve greater self-awareness and wholeness. Rather than viewing our shadow as purely negative, it can be seen as a source of growth, as it contains aspects of our personality that, if we don't look more deeply into, can negatively impact our lives. Understanding our shadow self allows us to recognise recurring patterns in our lives, especially those related to trauma, as it can show how our past experiences can influence our present behaviour and emotional responses.

Rather than being completely negative, the shadow self can be seen as a filing cabinet crammed with unexamined feelings, creative potentials, and repressed memories. By rejecting these parts of ourselves, we risk allowing them to control our thoughts and actions subconsciously, often leading to self-sabotage or destructive behaviours. Leaving these parts unexamined is kind of like leaving the filing cabinet in a mess (ok, no one really has a filing cabinet anymore but stay with me here!). If we leave this filing cabinet alone and it is full to the brim, the chances are that the drawer is going to keep popping open every time we walk past it. Lots of old paperwork (paperwork – what's that?!) might fall out, and we pick it up and stuff it back in and force the cabinet drawer closed with our foot. But if we were to open the filing cabinet, take out all of the paperwork that's been stuffed in there over the years, take a look at it, reorganise it and put it back in the cabinet in some sort of order, the chances are that the drawer will close properly and won't keep popping open every time we put a coffee mug on the top of it. Does that make sense? This is exactly the same as the emotions, traits and desires hidden in our shadow self. Your shadow self was ignored as a child, and probably never really understood by the people around you. This is why as an adult, your shadow self needs to be explored in order to be understood. A bit like the filing cabinet wants to be opened and reorganised so the drawer can finally close properly! An example of this would be somebody who experienced constant criticism as a child. This child may develop an inner belief of being unworthy and not good enough, leading their shadow to manifest as self-doubt and fear of failure in adulthood. Recognising that the shadow self originates in the experiences of the inner child can empower us to address these issues.

Naturally, we all want to avoid any uncomfortable emotions or memories, but ignoring them doesn't mean they disappear forever, they're more like a shark swimming under the surface, ready to bite us just when we least expect it! Our shadow self is the same, and it will inevitability lurk in the background and manifest in other ways including a low self-esteem, low mood, anxiety, self-sabotage, and difficulties in building and maintaining relationships with other people. If we reject our shadow selves, we might start projecting onto people around us. This happens when we recognise our own unacceptable or unlikable traits or impulses in somebody else in an attempt to avoid recognising them in ourselves. An example of this would be a person who criticises somebody else's appearance is most likely projecting their feelings of insecurity about their own appearance.

Things that you find irritating or frustrating about other people and parts of yourself that you reject often show us part of our shadow self. If as a child you were always told to be quiet and sit nicely and weren't allowed to run around and be free because you were told it was annoying, as an adult you may then dislike people who are loud or speak up or have an extroverted personality because you might see these traits as annoying. I'm hoping this is starting to make sense!

So, what is shadow work then? Shadow work is where we uncover those parts of ourselves that we try to repress and hide, and instead of feeling shame towards these parts of ourselves, we learn to develop a sense of understanding, compassion and acceptance. If particular parts of you were shamed during your childhood, shadow work enables us to take a closer look at these parts and look at how our shadow self influences our thoughts, emotions, behaviours and our relationships with both ourselves and others. It is only when we have an awareness of our shadow self that we can live as our true and authentic self. Shadow work enables us to improve our overall sense of wellbeing and allows us to truly love ourselves instead of constantly shaming ourselves. It allows us to bring ourselves back into balance and look at ourselves as a whole rather than avoiding certain parts of ourselves.

In our adult lives, we might engage in different strategies to try to avoid our shadow self at all costs!

These might include:

- Overworking – so we can avoid any negative beliefs about ourselves being lazy or not good enough.
- We might constantly overachieve and engage in perfectionist tendencies, again to negate any negative beliefs about ourselves not being good enough or not being worthy.
- We might also get into unhealthy relationships that make us feel good for a while, which improves our self-esteem and makes us feel worthy and loved for a period of time, but ultimately don't work out. Think of Dave always

replying to your messages, making you laugh, saying all the right things, never leaving you on read, and then suddenly he's sending one word responses the next day and keeps making excuses as to why he's busy and can't see you. Deep down, you know that Dave is treating you badly, but you stay with him because "when it's good it's really good!" And "he can be so nice"! Basically, we stay because the times we are made to feel loved and worthy seem more important than the times we cry ourselves to sleep.

If you notice yourself getting into these unhealthy patterns, it might be time to do some shadow work! One thing to know about shadow work is that it will hurt before you begin to heal. And I'm not going to lie to you here, it might hurt a lot. But don't let the pain stop you from you from doing the work you need to do in order to fully heal.

So how do we connect with our shadow selves? One way to connect with your shadow self is through journalling. This will allow you to ask yourself some questions which will help you to be able to fully reflect on your shadow self and any emotions you avoid.

Some questions you might want to ask yourself to connect with your shadow self are:

- What situations bring out the worst in you?
- What emotions bring out the worst in you?
- Think about your parents' best and worst traits – do you feel as though you have any of these traits?
- Are there any personality traits you wish you didn't have?
- Do you ever find yourself avoiding certain emotions?
- What emotions are these?

- What do you do to avoid these emotions?
- What scares you and why?
- Think about a time that someone let you down as a child – how did it feel, how did you react? Do you notice any of these same patterns now?

Another way to connect with your shadow self is to observe your reactions to situations. Let's say there is a situation which caused you to MASSIVELY overreact. Instead of retreating into yourself and wishing the ground would swallow you up after a completely irrational outburst, try showing yourself some kindness and compassion and taking a deeper look into the overreaction. Ask yourself what thoughts went through your mind, what emotions did you notice? Did those emotions show up for you in a physical sense? For example, did you have a knot in your stomach, did you feel sick, did you notice your heart racing? Then think about how this impacted your behaviour. What did you do as a response to this situation? Was there anything you purposely avoided? Did the emotions you felt remind you of another time in your life when you also felt these emotions? For example, getting disproportionately angry at your friend for cancelling on your Friday night plans because she has to work late might remind you of a time when you were younger and your parent or caregiver was always too busy to spend time with you. By taking a deeper look into an emotional response, you will be able to identify more about your shadow self and what triggers these responses. You will also be able to work out whether it was you who was angry, or whether it was actually your inner child in the driving seat (most often it's the latter!) and you'll be able to work out what it was your inner child needed at that time, so that if a similar situation arises in the future, you are able to tune into the emotions of your younger self and see what they need to hear. They might need to hear that this isn't a rejection and that they are still loved and wanted. This then brings the parts of our personality that we have supressed back into our consciousness, so that we are able to accept them and love them. Remember that if your reaction is hysterical, it comes from something historical.

It might also be that you are attaching a different meaning to the situation. If we use the previous example of our friend cancelling our plans, it might be that you attach the meaning that you are not good enough for people to want to spend time with, or perhaps you aren't fun or important enough, when actually the situation is probably exactly what she said it was, she genuinely had to work late! By identifying what meaning we are giving the situation, we are able to look at where that meaning comes from and ask ourselves whether that meaning is an accurate reflection of the current situation. Sometimes all we need is a day of self-reflection! Shadow work is all about taking responsibility and ownership for the parts of ourselves that we don't like, looking at them without judgement and using these parts to heal the wounded parts of our younger self.

Another way to do shadow work is to meditate. Many people aren't comfortable with the idea of sitting with themselves in silence. I mean, it is a bit awkward the first few times you do it! Sitting with your thoughts and emotions, observing them and not reacting or responding to them is difficult, but it is something we could all do with learning to do. I bet there are a few times in your life you wished you hadn't reacted straight away and just sat with your feelings until you had calmed down a bit. I know I have a few situations I can think of! Learning to meditate means that you will learn to be an observer to your thoughts and emotions instead of a reactor. By becoming the observer, you can watch what is going on without judgement, and you can be curious about it too. Ask yourself questions about how you are feeling and if this feeling reminds you of another time in your childhood. You could even incorporate visualisation techniques into your meditation, whereby you imagine your shadow self as a separate entity and talk to it. This enables you to engage and understand this part of yourself better, making it less intimidating.

Shadow work is beneficial to all of us, even if it is painful and uncomfortable. But pain and discomfort also help us to grow and teach us more about ourselves. Connecting with our shadow self enables us to have greater emotional regulation as we learn to look more deeply into the origins of our triggers and learn to handle difficult emotions more constructively. On the other hand, if we avoid our shadow self, we sort of become like Peter Pan and never grow up. Now as great as this seemed when we were kids, the idea of continuously reliving unhealthy patterns and not resolving our emotional baggage inevitably leads to a life of self-sabotaging and getting stuck in the same old cycles. Getting to know your shadow self might be difficult, it might be painful, but it also might be the best thing you ever do.

CHAPTER 8

The Inner Child and the Nervous System

U nderstanding the dynamics of our nervous system, particularly in relation to childhood trauma and emotional regulation, is imperative for both our healing and our personal development. Childhood trauma can have a huge impact on our nervous system, and when we understand the links between these, we can develop strategies for regulating our nervous systems and building a greater emotional resilience.

The nervous system is basically the part of our body that manages all of the crucial functions and keeps everything running smoothly.

It is divided into two main branches:

1. Central nervous system (CNS): This includes the brain and spinal cord and is responsible for processing information and coordinating responses.
2. Peripheral nervous system (PNS) which includes everything outside the CNS and connects the brain and the spinal cord to the rest of the body. The PNS is then divided into:

- The somatic nervous system which controls our voluntary movements (like moving our arms)
- The automatic nervous system (ANS) which regulates involuntary functions (like breathing and heart rate).

Now this is where it gets tricky, as Stephen Porges's (2011) Polyvagal theory states that the vagus nerve, which runs from our brain to various major organs in our body, doesn't just play a part in our physical functioning, but is also crucial in regulating our emotional and physiological responses, meaning that the ANS is then divided into a further three pathways. It proposes that responses to perceived threats – and the important word here is "perceived" – so whether it is an actual life or death situation, e.g. not looking as you cross the road and having a near miss with a passing car, rather than your boss sending you an email asking you to attend a meeting with them on Monday morning, occur in a hierarchical structure:

Ventral vagal complex (social engagement): This system is associated with feelings of safety, social engagement and calmness. The ventral vagal complex promotes behaviours that enhance social connection and emotional regulation. Whilst in this state you might feel relaxed and content and as though you are living in the present moment.

Sympathetic nervous system (fight/flight): The sympathetic nervous system is responsible for the body's fight or flight responses, activating physiological changes that prepare the body to face threats (whether they are real or perceived). Being in this state involves experiencing physical sensations such as an increased heart rate, rapid breathing, and increased blood flow to the muscles. You might feel as though you are on high alert, have too much energy and are shaky and fidgety.

Dorsal vagal complex (immobility): When faced with extreme stress, the dorsal vagal complex, another part of the parasympathetic nervous system, can lead to the "shutdown" responses. This can manifest as dissociation, numbness, or an inability to act. In this response you might notice that you have low energy, brain fog and difficulty focussing and speaking. Emotionally you might feel depressed and hopeless. While this response can be protective, it often connects deeply with patterns of trauma.

What has the nervous system got to do with childhood trauma?

Childhood trauma can lead to dysregulation in the automatic nervous system, making survivors more prone to sympathetic hyperactivation (anxiety and panic) or dorsal vagal shutdown (depression and dissociation). So, when people say that time is a healer (I hate that saying!) this isn't always true. When we experience a traumatic event, it actually leaves an imprint on our nervous system, which impacts how we see both the world and ourselves. After an event has passed, the sensations and emotions stay trapped in our body and can cause dysregulation which continues in our adult lives. The sympathetic branch of the ANS becomes overactive in people who have experienced childhood trauma, as their brains are constantly searching for threats and danger. This leaves them in a constant state of hypervigilance, meaning that situations which are not life or death (getting that message from your new partner saying "we need to talk"), feel the same as being chased by a lion! This can all lead to emotional challenges, difficulty forming relationships and an ongoing struggle to connect to the inner child. Recognising the signs of nervous system regulation is important if we want to recover from our past and heal our inner child.

Our ability to self-regulate our emotions is primarily based upon how we related to our parents in the early years of our lives. The more secure your attachment was to your parent or caregiver in the first few years of your life, the more able you will be to regulate your emotions. If we felt loved and had our needs met as a child, we build a level of trust with our parents which lets us know that we can rely on them and in turn creates a nervous system that is calm and regulated. In our adult life, we carry these early experiences and attachments with us, which set a kind of unconscious guide for how our emotions and physical sensations respond to certain situations in our lives. If we didn't have parents who attended to our needs, we were likely to have developed an insecure attachment type, meaning that we might struggle with anxiety and a dysregulated nervous system. This doesn't mean that if you had a difficult time growing up, you're completely screwed! Our ability to self-regulate will constantly change in our lives depending on our past experiences, our current circumstances, and the work we put into it.

There are many activities we can do to regulate our nervous system and engage our ventral vagal pathway to create a sense of emotional safety:

Deep breathing exercises: Practising diaphragmatic breathing can activate the vagus nerve, promoting a relaxation response. Take long, deep breaths, allowing your abdomen to expand and contract.

Mindfulness: Mindfulness is the practice of paying focussed, non-judgemental attention to the present moment. It involves being fully aware of your thoughts, feelings, bodily sensations, and the surrounding environment without trying to judge or change them. This practice helps promote a sense of calm, clarity, and emotional regulation, and is often used in techniques such as meditation, breathing exercises, and everyday activities to reduce stress and increase overall wellbeing. Mindfulness practices, such as guided meditations focussed on self-compassion and nurturing the inner child, can help promote inner child healing.

Play or be creative!: When we engage in playful and creative activities, we are connecting with our inner child on a deeper level. Ever noticed how you feel more at peace and carefree when you're playing with children or animals? Being playful and spontaneous is essential for nervous system regulation.

Being out in nature: Spending time outdoors and connecting with nature can have a calming effect on the nervous system. Activities such as hiking, gardening or simply walking in a park can help ground us.

Gentle movement practices: Yoga, tai chi, or other forms of gentle movement can help create a sense of connection to the body and activate the vagus nerve.

Create a safe space in your mind: Build a space in your mind you can retreat to when things get too much. It could be anywhere you feel safe and calm, perhaps the beach at your favourite holiday destination or a beach built purely from your imagination. It could be somewhere you felt safe as a child, or even a park bench, imagining the warm breeze on your face. It will take time and repetition but once you have your safe space, you can go there whenever you need to.

Look for glimmers: Glimmers are the opposite of triggers, so just as a trigger evokes a negative emotional response, a glimmer is something that creates a sense of calmness and safety. A glimmer could be anything from spending time with a particular friend, it might be a particular place, or it might even be a stranger who smiled at you in the corner shop.

Humming: The vibration created by humming actually stimulates the vagus nerve which in turn activates the parasympathetic nervous system which provides a sense of relaxation. So next time someone gives you a funny look when you're humming to yourself in the office, tell them you're calming your nervous system!

This is by far my favourite…laugh!: Being around people who make you laugh, watching your favourite funny film or stand-up comedian can stimulate the vagus nerve and provides a sense of relaxation which improves our mood.

There are so many other regulating activities, I could go on forever! Having a bath, listening to your favourite music, reading a book or EFT tapping are also some great go-to strategies for regulating your nervous system. Something that you might find useful is to have a think about your favourite regulating activities and make a list of your top four or five. Then, when you're feeling anxious, stressed or just generally dysregulated, you can go to your list and pick the one you feel like doing and the one that is most appropriate for the time and place you find yourself in. For example, going for a walk might be one of your regulating activities but you might not want to go outside if it's chucking it down! So, you might choose to read a book instead. If you're feeling dysregulated driving to work, you can put on your favourite music (because I wouldn't recommend reading a book and driving – although you could listen to an Audiobook!). Make your list your own and make sure you go to it when you need it!

So next time you're feeling as though your entire world is coming crashing down over something that your rational self knows isn't life or death, remember that it's just your nervous system in dysregulation and the voice of your inner child crying out for attention and healing. If we learn to acknowledge these feelings from inside of us instead of dismissing them, we can use them as an opportunity to grow and heal, and by doing so, we don't only reclaim our emotional resilience, but we will also empower our inner child and help her to thrive.

PART TWO
THE PROBLEMS AND STRATEGIES

CHAPTER 9

Goals aren't just for New Years!

We've all been there on December 31st...every year. We make so many resolutions, plans, goals, things we want to do, see, achieve in the new year. And this year we really mean it, it's not like last year! Last year was a write off, this year is the real thing, we're really going to do everything we've set ourselves to do! At the start of January, we really mean what we say! We begin the year with good intentions, we eat healthily, we get that gym membership we've been going on about for ages, and we are NOT going to let Dave, or any other Dave, walk all over us. Before we know it, we're two weeks into the year, sat on the sofa with a Domino's and Ben & Jerry's, repeatedly checking our phone to see if we have had any form of correspondence from Dave. Suddenly, December 31st feels as though it was a million years ago.

So, let's take a deeper look into goals and see what changes we can fashion to make goal setting a bit easier and well...realistic!

Most of us have some sort of goal we want to achieve. We can set goals in different areas of our life including:

- Environmental – you might want to change something about the environment you are in, whether it's moving or making changes to your current home or environment.
- Career – you might want a new job or a promotion, or maybe you want to start something new altogether.

- Finances – you might want to pay off some debt or save some more money by a certain date.
- Physical health – you may want to improve your physical health or fitness, this could be anything from exercising more to improving strength, losing weight, or eating more healthily.
- Relationships – you may aim to spend more time with loved ones, meet new friends, set more boundaries.
- Mental health/personal growth – you might want to improve your confidence or focus more on positives rather than worrying or ruminating.

Although we might know what it is we want, it might feel as though every time we try to move towards that goal, something gets in our way. Quite often whatever it is that is getting in our way can be related to our childhood, even though we might not realise it. For example, our childhood might have led us to develop negative core beliefs about ourselves, leaving us to believe things like "I'm not good enough" or "I don't deserve to succeed". These beliefs about ourselves often stem from critical voices we encountered in our younger years and become a self-fulfilling prophecy, as if we believe we aren't good enough, we probably won't put 100% into our goals, or maybe we won't even try at all.

But just because there was a time you didn't win the 100 metre sprint at Sports Day, it does NOT mean you're a failure. When thinking about something you want to achieve, it might bring up some unwanted thoughts and emotions from the past. Perhaps there was even a time not too long ago when you set yourself something you wanted to achieve, and you didn't meet your goal. Maybe you remember how it made you feel and don't want to feel the same again. We can quite easily get ourselves into negative patterns and habits if we try and avoid anything that might involve bringing up upsetting emotions. If you ever feel like this, ask yourself whether it's the goal you are avoiding, or whether it is actually the negative emotions you are avoiding. Notice what comes up for you when you think about working towards that goal. What thoughts come up, how do you feel in your body? Remind yourself that that was then, and this is now. Just because you haven't achieved a goal you set yourself before, it does not mean that you can't achieve a goal you set yourself now. And it definitely does NOT make you a failure. Remind yourself of the times where you have achieved things, no matter how little. Doing this will get you into a more positive headspace and will change your focus of attention away from the negatives.

In addition, our childhood experiences can lead to a fear of failure. If we were criticised harshly as a child or if we were made to feel as though we never met anybody's expectations, we might then grow into adults who avoid setting goals all together, as we might be scared that we will never be able to achieve them. Furthermore, many adults who carry unresolved childhood trauma struggle with imposter syndrome, meaning that they feel undeserving of their achievements and think that it is somehow a fluke that they ended up where they are now. This in turn can also prevent people from setting and pursuing goals.

Understanding the cycle between the beliefs created in our childhood and our goals is important. Our beliefs about ourselves shape our aspirations and in turn, our goals influence our self-concept. For example, if we believe we are unworthy of success we might set minimal goals or none at all, leading us to feel stuck in a rut.

If we want to break this cycle, we need to reflect on our childhood experiences and their impact on how we feel in our adult life. We also need to recognise situations that trigger feelings of inadequacy so that we are better able to connect with our inner child and address these triggers.

Once we begin to address our inner child and the beliefs tied to our past, we can start setting goals that are not only achievable, but that are also aligned with our true selves. The SMART (Specific, Measurable, Achieveable, Relevant, Time-bounded) framework (if you use this at work, don't roll your eyes!) is a useful tool for setting goals.

Specific: Clearly define what it is you want to achieve. If for example your goal is, "I want to be happier", it can be helpful to think about what your life would look like if you felt happier, for example, what would you be doing differently? Would you be doing more for yourself, or starting a new hobby? Would you be more confident in being assertive and being able to say no to things that you don't want to do? Would you be spending more time with your friends or family? Thinking that your goal in life is to be happy is great, but ask yourself what happy actually means to you. Another example is "I want to be healthier". Instead of this, your goal could be to exercise three times a week.

Measurable: Setting criteria for measuring progress. For example, tracking your workouts, identifying how much money you want to have saved by a certain date etc.

Achievable: Now here's the thing, when we set a goal, we usually think about the big end goal, which is great, we know what we want to get to, but often what we don't do is think about what small steps we can take to get there. Think about when you want to achieve this goal by. Is it a few months, a year, or more? Let's say for argument's sake that this particular goal will take you a year to achieve, what is a smaller goal you can set for six months that will help you towards the end goal? And then what is a three-month goal that will help you get towards the six-month goal? A monthly goal to get towards the three-month goal. And what can you do every week to make sure you get to that monthly goal? I usually describe this to my clients as a timeline, where we are at the start and the end goal is at the end, but we have to fill in the smaller steps in the middle. Breaking big goals down into smaller more achievable steps will give us a more positive mindset that this goal is actually achievable and within our reach, and with every small step we feel a sense of achievement, which will give us more motivation to continue working towards the end goal.

Relevant: Make sure you align your goals with your values and long-term aspirations. There is no point in making a goal to run a marathon if your idea of a run is seeing how quickly you can get your next snack during the advert break (definitely my idea of a sprint!). If your goal doesn't align with your true self, it will feel more like a chore than a challenge.

Time-bounded: Make sure you set yourself a deadline for the time you want to achieve your goal. Procrastination won't get you anywhere! It is also important to check in on the progress of your goals. Depending on when it is you want to achieve your goal by, you might want to set check-in dates to ensure that you are still on track to meet your goal. Something you might want to ask yourself is "what can I do today/this week" that will help me get closer towards my goal?". By ensuring that your goal is at the forefront of your mind, you are more likely to take small steps to ensure that you achieve it.

When working towards your goals, if something goes wrong, don't beat yourself up and immediately give up, but be compassionate with yourself, just like you would a friend. If a friend wanted to give up on something they wanted to achieve because they thought they couldn't do it, would you a) tell them to give up and agree that they aren't going to achieve it anyway or b) encourage them not to give up and help them problem solve ways they can achieve their goal? Let's be honest, the answer is most likely the second option! When we are kind to ourselves and talk to our younger self in the same way that we would talk to a friend, we usually find that we feel more motivated and have more belief in ourselves.

When it comes to setting and achieving goals, remember that understanding and healing our inner child can be a vital part of the process. Our childhood experiences and core beliefs often shape our perceptions of what we think is possible for ourselves. By being compassionate with ourselves and confronting these deep-seated beliefs, we can create and achieve more authentic and fulfilling goals. So be kind to yourself, don't give up, and get to work!

Top tips for goal setting:

1. STOP giving up at the first hurdle. If plan A doesn't work, there are 25 more letters in the alphabet!

2. DO be clear and specific about what it is you want to achieve and work out what smaller steps you can take to get there.
3. And finally DUMP the unrealistic goals! Don't start something in January that you know full well you won't be doing in March!

CHAPTER 10

Don't EVER lower your worth because Dave can't afford it

Yes, exactly what I just said. Don't lower your self-worth because Dave can't afford it. But before we look at lowering your worth, let's first start off by looking at what self-worth is in the first place. We always hear people talking about it, but what exactly does it mean?

Self-worth is a feeling or sense of being good enough and valuing yourself. It is knowing that you have value and that you deserve to be treated in a certain way, and that you deserve respect. Our sense of worth may stem from our childhood. If we grew up in a stable home with parents who praised us, showed us affection and attention, and always supported us and showed us unconditional love, we are likely to have a high self-worth. If as children, we were shown that we are worthy of love and respect and don't need to achieve certain things or be something or someone we are not to receive it, we are less likely to believe that we need to do certain things or have achieved certain things to be worthy of love and respect as an adult.

However, if we grew up in a household where we were criticised, not shown love or affection, shown love that was conditional depending on our achievements or behaviour, or made to feel as though our emotions were silly or not important, we are more likely to have a lower self-worth. As adults, we are more likely to believe that we need to do or achieve certain things in order to be loved and respected, and therefore become people pleasers. This subconscious idea of our worth or value as a child gets carried through to our adulthood and determines what behaviour we do and don't accept from people around us. The lower our self-worth, the more likely we are to put up with crappy behaviour from other people (yes, you, Dave!) because we subconsciously don't think we are worth any more than this.

So the question is, do you have self-worth? And if you do, how much? When thinking about your self-worth, try asking yourself some questions such as:

- Do you like yourself?
- How much do you like yourself? There's a difference between liking yourself a little bit and liking yourself a lot!
- How would you describe yourself to someone who has never met you?
- Do you believe that you are worthy of the love and respect from people around you?

When you're thinking about the answers to these questions, be as honest as you can. If you don't like yourself a great deal and don't believe you are worthy of love and respect, the chances are you might have a low self-worth. You might have a fear of failure or you might worry about being criticised. You might have difficulty accepting compliments from other people as you struggle to believe they are genuine. The reason that people with low self-worth often find themselves engaging in people-pleasing behaviours is that they get their validation through doing things for others as they are not able to give it to themselves. This means that their needs aren't met as they constantly strive to meet the needs of others around them. In addition, they might find it difficult to stand up for themselves and act like…well…a door mat. Does any of this sound familiar?

Sometimes we relate our self-worth to our possessions (having a nice car, house, etc) or the things we have achieved (what we do for work, how educated we are, how many marathons we have run etc). However, what happens when we can no longer afford our nice new car and have to get an older one? What happens if we are made redundant or don't beat our best time training for that marathon in six months? As soon as these things happen, we feel as if we have failed or that we have lost the approval of others around us, and our self-worth hits an all-time low.

When we have a low self-worth, we are likely to get into relationships or stay in relationships that we probably wouldn't stay in if our self-worth was higher. Let's talk about Dave. When you first met Dave, he was nice, funny, listened to you, replied to your messages in a timely manner (always important!), told you how beautiful you are and generally always made seeing you a priority. Now it's a few months in, and his standards are slipping. He leaves you on read and replies to your messages as and when he sees fit, sometimes only gives you a "lol" or a thumbs up emoji, and he's making excuses as to why he can't see you.

Is his behaviour good enough?

No.

Do you tolerate it?

Probably.

Why?

What stops you from telling him to either get his act together or get on his bike? Why are you so afraid of losing someone who isn't treating you the way you should be treated? Is it because when it's good it's really good? Is it because he makes you feel like nobody else ever has? Is it because every time you think there's a red flag, there's always something to explain it? And sometimes there are genuine reasons for somebody's behaviour, but don't make the mistake of being so understanding that you overlook the fact that you are not being treated with the respect you deserve. When somebody consistently treats you in a way that is less than you deserve, even after you have tried to discuss it with them, it's time to start asking yourself why you are allowing it. Would you rather tolerate Dave's crap because you don't want to lose him, or would you rather tell him to jog on because you don't want to lose yourself?

When we start tolerating unacceptable behaviour, we are immediately lowering our value and letting that person know that it's ok for them to treat us this way. Think about it in terms of a shop. There is a high price item on the top shelf that is only going to go to people who are able to pay the right price for it. Then we've got the sale shelf, where the more affordable items are that the majority of people will be able to pay for. Imagine you start out on the top shelf, you value yourself and you're only getting off of that shelf if the right person comes along and treats you in the way you deserve (i.e. the person who can afford the high ticket item on the top shelf). But if somebody comes along and offers less, and you accept that, you might as well have put yourself on the sale shelf to begin with where anyone can pay (in the metaphorical sense!) what they like and you accept it. Remember that you have worth, you have value and make sure you put yourself on the top shelf and only come off of that shelf for somebody worthy who can truly afford you. There will come a time when you finally realise your worth, and when you do, you won't be interested in anyone who can't see it.

If after reflecting on this you feel as though your self-worth needs to be improved, you're probably wondering where you even start with that! There are a few things you can start doing that will help to improve your self-worth.

- Think about things you value in life: What do you value in life? Your family, friends, hobbies, career, your health? Think about whether you are living in line with those values, and if you aren't, ask yourself what you can do to work more towards those values. For example, if you value being a good friend, are you putting enough into your friendships, or have you been so busy with work lately that you just haven't got around to sending your friend a message to see how she is. If one of your values is being fit and healthy, are you living in line with this, or have you been skipping your exercise routine lately because you're feeling miserable after Dave's latest crap and instead of your usual healthy eating you've been indulging in too much fast food? We all do this, and there isn't a problem with it if that's what works for you, but if you notice that you're not living by your values and that this is starting to impact your mood, you might decide that you want to make a change.

- Challenge your unhelpful thoughts: If you notice yourself having negative thoughts about yourself, remember that a thought is just a thought, and not necessarily a fact. Ask yourself what evidence you have got that goes against that thought and replace the unhelpful thought with a more balanced, realistic thought (see chapter on overthinking!).

- Use positive affirmations: In order to help yourself get out of unhelpful patterns of thinking, try using positive affirmations on a regular basis and notice the difference in how you feel after using them consistently for a period of time (you might want to take a look at the chapter on positive affirmations!).

- Forgive yourself: Stop beating yourself up over past mistakes. Feeling angry with ourselves over things that have happened in the past will impact whatever we are trying to do in the present. If you keep beating yourself up over that mistake you made at work last week, how are you supposed to be completely present and focussed this week? If you keep remembering that mistake you made in a past relationship, how can you ever be present in your current relationship and make sure that you are the best that you can be? We need to acknowledge what happened in the past, ask ourselves what we can learn from it, and then move forward with our lives.

- Accept yourself: Accept yourself for who you are and stop comparing yourself to other people. Quite often we think about all of the positives of people around us and forget about our own positives. Embrace yourself for who you are. Remember you are one of a kind, you don't need to change for anyone.

When it comes to our self-worth, remember that it is not determined by our external circumstances, others' opinions, and certainly do not let Dave's actions make you feel as though you aren't worthy! Healing is a process, not a destination. Although your low self-worth stems from past wounds, it doesn't have to define your future, and every effort you make to treat yourself with kindness, patience and understanding is a step towards rewiring those old beliefs. Remember that you are always enough, just as you are.

Top tips for managing low self-worth:

1. STOP accepting behaviour that isn't good enough for you because you feel as though you aren't good enough. Remind yourself that you ARE good enough.
2. DO work on improving your self-worth by living in line with your values and practising self-acceptance and self-forgiveness.
3. And finally, DUMP anyone who treats you with less respect and love than you deserve!

CHAPTER 11
Self-sabotage

S omething that I often hear from my clients is that they know something they are doing isn't good for them, but they still keep doing it. It could also be that they aren't doing something which they know would be good for them, but they still just don't do it. I'm sure we can all relate to that! If I had a pound for every time I said I was going to give up chocolate, or get up an hour earlier and get a good exercise routine into place, I would be ridiculously rich! Whatever it is, we've all been there. There's often a sense of frustration that comes with getting stuck into these unhealthy patterns, even if we know what we're doing. We might feel angry at ourselves that we are still doing that thing, or seeing that person, or in that relationship/friendship, when we know we would be better off not doing it. Equally, we might feel a sense of frustration or annoyance at ourselves when we're not doing something, whether it's eating healthily, looking for a new job or going to the gym. These behaviours are known as self-sabotaging behaviours and they refer to when we consciously or unconsciously prevent ourselves from achieving our goals, or when we do something that has a negative impact on our wellbeing. Self-sabotaging behaviours range from drinking, taking drugs, self-medicating, procrastinating, perfectionism and more.

These behaviours stem from behaviours that were useful at one point in our lives but aren't anymore. We may have had certain experiences in our childhood which formed beliefs about helpful and unhelpful behaviours. For example, if we had parents who gave us attention if we became angry and shouted and screamed, we may learn that in order to get attention as adults, we need to shout and scream. However, as adults we know that this isn't a helpful response when we are in the working environment or in an adult relationship, and these behaviours can become extremely damaging to our lives very quickly.

When we self-sabotage, it is often a coping mechanism which is used to protect us from low self-esteem, a fear of change or a fear of failure. If we deliberately sabotage something, it feels better than being told by somebody else that we have failed. For example, if you tried really hard to study for an exam you had coming up and put all of your effort into it, how would you feel if you didn't achieve what you wanted to achieve? Disappointed? Frustrated? Like a failure? Whereas if you deliberately procrastinate and put off your revision, knowing full well that you really need to do it, it would come as less of a shock to you if you failed. You wouldn't be as disappointed as you would have already been expecting it, which leaves us with a "well I knew that would happen anyway" attitude. After all, you can't fail if you don't try!

Another reason we self-sabotage is that self-sabotaging makes a situation predictable, which gives us the illusion of control. As a child, if we grew up in an environment with parents who were controlling, and we didn't feel able to show our emotions or do anything that was seen as "wrong" due to the fear of being punished, then it makes sense that we would try to gain a feeling of control as an adult. An example of this could be being in a relationship which is good for you, but sabotaging it because you think it will end up going wrong anyway. If you had a difficult relationship with a parent when you were growing up, you might have developed core beliefs of "I'm unloveable", which again leads to self-sabotaging in relationships as you might not feel that it is possible for anyone to love you. By sabotaging the relationship, this reinforces your negative core beliefs and keeps you trapped in this unhelpful cycle.

Alternatively, you might have a habit of getting into relationships with people who aren't right for you and don't treat you very well. You may notice that these people have similar traits (or if you haven't noticed, I'm sure you have that friend who has pointed it out to you!). Sometimes it might feel easier to keep choosing similar relationships, as they are predictable, and we already know how it will play out from the start. This prevents us from having to sit through that feeling of uncertainty and not knowing what will happen.

So how do we get out of the cycle of self-sabotage? Well first of all ask yourself, what would happen if you were to take a risk and do something different? If we think about this in terms of relationships and not going for your usual Dave who you know will ultimately let you down, how would it feel to be with somebody different to the norm? Scary? Unknown? Would you feel more vulnerable? Would you feel more hurt if it didn't work out? Sometimes the fear of being with somebody who is good for us feels like it's more of a risk as we have more to lose. Whereas if we get into similar relationships with similar people, we might not necessarily get our hopes up from the beginning, which prevents us from getting as hurt.

The same goes for careers and jobs. Have you ever stopped yourself from applying for a job you really want because you don't believe you're good enough for it? So instead you have stayed in a job you can't stand and isn't challenging enough for you because you're scared of being rejected, so you self-sabotage by not even applying in the first place. The truth is, although we don't intend to do things that make us feel worse or take us further away from our goals, our natural state is to go back to the feeling we are used to feeling, just because it's familiar. And familiarity is safety, even if it isn't helpful for us in the long term. We revert back to self-sabotaging behaviours because we can predict what's coming, which makes us feel more in control of the situation. This keeps us stuck in old patterns that are predictable, feel safe, and make us feel less vulnerable. But if we take a risk and do something different, yes, we might feel anxious, yes, we might feel more vulnerable, yes, it feels unknown, BUT, what if it actually works out? What if this relationship that you're too scared to be vulnerable for is actually the right one? What if you get that job and it's actually your dream job? Too often we think about all the things that might go wrong, but forget to ask ourselves, what if it doesn't and we've missed out on that opportunity because of our fears? Sometimes in life we have to make the jump and take a risk because it might just work out. And well, if it doesn't, at least you won't look back wondering "what if?".

Another way to break the cycle of self-sabotage is to identify your triggers. Keep a journal of the moments when you recognise your self-sabotaging tendencies. Maybe you notice you completely lose it with your partner for something you know deep down isn't a good reason, or perhaps you avoid something at work because you think you'll fail anyway. Reflect on what it was that actually triggered your reactions in these situations. By recognising your triggers, you will be more able to understand them, prepare for them, and connect with your inner child to reassure her that everything is ok.

In addition, it is helpful to pay attention to your negative self-talk which reinforces feelings of inadequacy and fear. So next time you hear your critical inner voice telling you that you aren't good enough for whatever it is you want to do, or not good enough for a certain person, make sure that you challenge your negative thoughts by questioning their validity and reframing them in a more positive light. Ask yourself whether these thoughts are based on facts or whether they are simply reflections of past experiences and fears. Instead of accepting the belief that you aren't good enough, think about situations in your life where you have succeeded in something, been proud of something you did, or received positive feedback or compliments. This process of reframing helps to shift your perspective, allowing you to recognise your strengths and capabilities which will help you refrain from self-sabotaging.

Ultimately, self-sabotage is often a manifestation of unresolved childhood trauma and unmet needs. Understanding this connection and actively paying attention to and nurturing our inner child can help us to heal and to grow, which in turn will stop us in our tracks when we begin to self-sabotage and help us get into healthier cycles. So, stop self-sabotaging, apply for the job, start the hobby, and dump any Daves who aren't good enough!

Top tips to stop self-sabotaging:

1. STOP getting into the same patterns that you know aren't helpful for you just because they feel safer.
2. DO try to accept that you can't be in control of every situation.
3. DUMP the negative core beliefs that are leading you to self-sabotage in the first place, and remember you are worthy, you are loveable, you are good enough!

CHAPTER 12

Toxic Shame

Toxic shame isn't just that "oh shit" feeling after tripping up the stairs in front of your work colleagues – and let's be honest, we've all been there! It's that deep, nagging voice that tells you that there's something very wrong with you. Shame can often be confused with guilt, but it goes a step further, as this nagging voice constantly tells you that you're unlovable, broken or flawed in some way, and guess what…it's all your fault.

Just imagine walking around with a post-it note on your forehead that says "I'm not good enough". Imagine how uncomfortable you would feel in your normal daily routine; talking to friends, colleagues, or even strangers who could all see the post-it note. Toxic shame becomes the lens through which we view ourselves and distorts our self-worth, which in turn has an impact on our thoughts, behaviours, and relationships.

Toxic shame often stems from negative childhood experiences. One possible cause of toxic shame is parents who may have unintentionally imposed impossibly high standards, leaving you feeling as though you have to earn their love, affection and approval. You might have grown up hearing things like "why can't you be more like your sister". This kind of comparison can create feelings of shame deep in a child's psyche and has an undeniable influence on how they feel about themselves both in their childhood and adult life.

Furthermore, you might have been frequently punished or criticised as a child, leaving you with a deep sense of shame and a feeling of not being good enough. You might have felt as though everything you did was wrong in some way and might have been belittled, shamed or ridiculed for making small mistakes. Klein (1991) described this experience as "some form of ridicule, scorn, contempt, or other degrading treatment at the hands of others". This in turn often leaves children feeling powerless and angry at how they have been treated, but as they aren't able to express their anger due to a fear of being punished by their parent or caregiver, the anger stays inside and manifests itself as toxic shame. The child then ends up becoming highly critical of themselves and takes on a sense of responsibility over whatever they have done "wrong" and ends up believing that they are flawed and undeserving of love. This can lead to children trying to people-please in order to feel loved, wanted and accepted. And guess what, children who learn to people-please become adults who people-please.

A further root cause of toxic shame can be bullying and negative peer interactions. Let's be honest, kids can be little a**holes at times – we all had that one person at school we dreaded running into in the corridor. You might have been bullied or had negative comments made about your clothes or appearance which have stuck with you throughout your adult life. As adults, we might find it easier to shake these sorts of comments off, but as children we are often more susceptible to criticism and believe that these sorts of comments are a true reflection of ourselves, rather than the person who made them.

Societal expectations can be another cause of toxic shame. I am lucky enough to remember growing up without social media, and an internet that I could only use for half an hour a day when somebody wasn't on the landline. If you're 30+ you will be able to relate! If you're under 30 you're probably wondering what the hell a landline is! With the ever-growing advancement in technology, we now have everything at the tip of our fingers (or thumbs!) making it easier to compare our lives, looks and relationships to other peoples, leaving us with a deep sense of shame over what we haven't got or haven't achieved. This sort of comparison is never helpful and just leaves us feeling completely and utterly crap about ourselves. It can be helpful to pay attention to how much time you spend on social media and notice how it is making you feel. If you can see that it's having an impact on your mood or how you feel about yourself, it might be time to reduce it a bit.

If you experience toxic shame, you'll probably already know that it can really screw with your adult life. Firstly, you might have a low self-esteem and may often feel worthless and inadequate. As an adult, you may find yourself avoiding challenges because you fear failure. You might think "What if I try and totally embarrass myself?". You might also be very self-critical and worry about what other people think, which again might lead to you just avoiding things all together. When it comes to avoiding things, you'll never know if you don't try, and you're probably not as bad at things as you think!

Many adults with toxic shame swing to the opposite end of the spectrum and become perfectionists. It's like trying to win a race but constantly stopping to check if your shoelaces are tied perfectly, or worse, giving up because "what's the point?". If you can't do it flawlessly, why do it at all? This often leads to self-sabotaging and giving up on opportunities or relationships before we even try.

Speaking of self-sabotage, toxic shame can lead to self-sabotaging pretty much everything. Ever been on a healthy eating kick and suddenly found yourself in the McDonald's drive thru ordering a Big Mac and large fries because "I'll just ruin it anyway"? That's self-sabotage at its finest! Toxic shame can create a cycle where we undermine our achievements and settle for less than we deserve because we think we aren't worthy of success or happiness.

Toxic shame can often lead to difficulties in relationships. It can lead to a fear of intimacy, where you might even hide your real self because you worry that if somebody really knew you then they will leave. There is often a fear of being seen and being vulnerable that arises from toxic shame, which leads to people withdrawing from those close to them, both physically and emotionally. This is often a survival mechanism, as if you had to hide your true self growing up, it makes sense that you wouldn't feel safe in being who you really are as an adult. This can lead to being stuck in survival mode and going through fight, flight and freeze reactions in relationships in order to prevent being traumatised or humiliated even more. However, even though you are trying to protect yourself, these behaviours become destructive as they lead to building emotional walls which create disconnected relationships and a never-ending cycle of miscommunication.

So now we know a bit more about toxic shame and how it can affect us, the question is, what the hell can we do about it?!

The first step to alleviating toxic shame is to acknowledge it and recognise that it exists. Thinking "I feel…" and naming the emotion is essential as it allows us to externalise and validate our experiences rather than internalising them. We then need to recognise the trigger by asking ourselves "where did this come from?". Ask yourself if you recognise this emotion from an earlier time in your life. How old does this emotion feel? Does it feel like seven-year-old-you when you were punished for accidentally breaking something whilst playing? When you have discovered where it has come from, challenge your thoughts about it in the current situation. For example, if you were punished and criticised for accidentally breaking something as a child, you might notice the same emotions if you make a mistake as an adult – for example a work colleague pointing out that you have made a small mistake. This small mistake might be absolutely nothing and easily corrected, but if you experienced trauma and shame as a child, this might lead you into a spiral of negative thoughts such as "they think I'm stupid" or catastrophising and thinking "I'm going to lose my job". When this happens, really challenge these thoughts and ask yourself if you have any evidence for them. Are there other work colleagues who have made mistakes and haven't lost their job? Is it really realistic that you will lose your job over something small? Once you have done this, try and reframe your thinking and create a more positive, helpful thought. It might be something like, "everyone makes mistakes and now I have learnt something new from this".

Secondly, practise self-compassion and treat yourself as you would a best friend who's going through a difficult time if you're experiencing feelings of toxic shame. You wouldn't say, "Get over it, you loser; nobody loves you!", would you? When we begin to speak to ourselves with kindness and understanding, we start to see our positives instead of just our flaws. Being compassionate with ourselves helps us to feel less isolated and soothes our nervous systems. Self-compassion goes a long way in redefining our narratives and making us think differently and feel better about ourselves.

Another way to heal toxic shame is by using visualisation techniques. Think of the most shameful experience in your childhood, and visualise your adult self speaking to your younger self. Tell your younger self what you needed to hear at that time. If you were humiliated, criticised or punished as a child, this would have led to extreme feeling of shame, so imagine you had a guardian angel there at the time and think about how they would have spoken to you and told you that this wasn't your fault and that you were still loved no matter what.

Sharing your story with somebody close to you can also help alleviate the feelings of shame. If there is somebody you trust and feel comfortable with, tell them the most shameful experience of your childhood. This could be a friend, partner or therapist. Opening up about these experiences can bring a sense of relief and validation, showing that you are not alone in your feelings.

In addition, skills such as mindfulness and grounding techniques (see chapter on overthinking for grounding techniques!) can help manage extreme emotional responses associated with toxic shame. These techniques can help create a sense of safety and make us feel more in control of our emotional responses.

Understanding that toxic shame is rooted in our past experiences and not our true selves is the first step toward healing. By recognising these feelings, we can begin to separate our identity from the hurtful narratives that were inflicted on us in our childhood. Healing involves compassion, self-awareness and often, seeking support to release these burdens. Remember, toxic shame is a result of what happened to you; it isn't who you are.

Top tips for managing toxic shame:

1. STOP giving attention to every unhelpful thought or memory, it will only drag you down!
2. DO be kind to yourself and speak to yourself like you would a friend. Make sure you ask yourself whether all of your negative and shameful thoughts about yourself are true.
3. DUMP the self-sabotage and avoidance. It will only get you stuck in a never-ending cycle of not feeling good enough.

CHAPTER 13

Perfectionism

J ust imagine this. You're a little girl and you've just done what you think is the most amazing painting. You've used your favourite colours; you've painted a big yellow sun and a bright blue sky with pink dots on (because why the hell not!). You go to show your loving (but critical) parent who tells you "that's not how you paint a sky, a sky doesn't have pink dots!". From this moment, you learn that your value is based on doing things the "right" way, and that there is only one right way to do things.

Perfectionism often starts out with adults in our lives wanting to mould us into something they deem as "acceptable". And whilst their intentions might be good, it can have a detrimental impact on the rest of our lives. When we are criticised for small mistakes or merely doing things differently as a child, we begin to associate love, validation and worthiness with performance. This teaches us that love is conditional and based on what we do rather than who we are. Perhaps there was a time when you got 100% on a test or came first in a competition and you were showered with love and attention? But the time you came second or third in that competition, the reaction just wasn't the same? This might have left you constantly striving for that first place or to never make a mistake again in your life, as if you do everything perfectly, you'll be shown that unconditional love and affection again. And who doesn't want that?

Perfectionism can also be a result of being punished for making mistakes as a child. This could be in the form of a physical punishment, withdrawing love or affection, being shouted at or being given the silent treatment. As children, this then leaves us with a sense of shame and a deep-seated belief that we are unworthy or inadequate in some way. You might have learnt that doing things perfectly was a good strategy to avoid someone's negative behaviour towards you. If you do everything perfectly, surely nobody could ever be angry with you? In essence, perfectionism is a trauma response which prevents us from feeling the same shame, criticism and rejection again.

Fast forward to adulthood and suddenly you're stuck in a cycle where anything less than perfect feels like an utter failure and you have zero tolerance for mistakes. You get sucked into an endless cycle of analysis paralysis whereby you're over-analysing every detail, constantly second guessing yourself and worrying that you're going to buy the wrong air fryer. Basically, doing everything perfectly and being in control is a pretty much guaranteed way to make your inner child feel safe.

So, what are the problems with being a perfectionist? Well firstly, can you ever have an off day if you're a perfectionist? Not usually, because if you do have a bad day, all of the negative core beliefs you hold about yourself rise to the surface and tell you how much of a failure you are. Didn't check that email you sent to your boss 17 times before sending it? You're definitely a failure. You accidently cut your child's sandwich into squares when they actually wanted triangles? You're a terrible parent. You didn't reply to your friend's message as soon as you saw it because you were up to your neck in it in that new work project? You're not a good enough friend.

And also, does doing everything perfectly ever make you feel satisfied or do you still end up feeling not good enough? Or maybe the more you try to control everything the more worried you feel about something going wrong?

How do you know if you're a perfectionist? Well here are some red flags to look for:

Procrastination: You tell yourself you're just being careful, but let's be honest, you're terrified of that email not being perfect so you spend half an hour re-reading it and triple checking the spellings just in case you've missed something.

Fear of failure: You would rather avoid any situation where you might mess up than face the absolute horror of doing something imperfectly.

Overanalysing: You spend three weeks deciding on the best mascara to get.

People pleasing: Your life mission is to make everyone happy, even at the expense of your own happiness.

Comparison trap: Constantly comparing your life to whoever you follow on social media. Newsflash – their life probably isn't as perfect as they'd like you to think!

So, how do we heal from perfectionism that resulted from childhood trauma?

- Acceptance: We need to acknowledge and accept our perfectionism. Accepting that this part of you exists and it's ok. You wouldn't criticise a friend for their perfectionism, so treat yourself like a friend!

- Connect with your inner child: You can use whatever method you prefer, whether it's journalling or visualisation, but have a heart-to-heart with your younger self and listen to what they have to say. Perhaps there was a specific time when you were a child when you were criticised for doing something "wrong" that has stuck with you, or maybe it was relentless criticism from a critical parent that has made you feel as though everything you do needs to be perfect. Tell her that it's okay to be imperfect, to fail and to learn. Let her know that no matter what, you will always love her and be there for her, even if she makes mistakes.

- Set realistic goals: Instead of aiming for perfection, aim for progress. Break your tasks into manageable goals and celebrate small victories. You finally cleaned out your wardrobe? Treat yourself to that Galaxy bar!

- Challenge your inner critic: When your brain tells you that you need to do everything perfectly, because if you don't, you're not good enough, ask yourself if that's actually true. Try to recognise what's driving the perfectionism. Is it the fear of being judged? Or maybe you're still trying to live up to impossibly high standards that were set for you as a child. Whatever it is, try to challenge those negative thoughts. If it's the fear of being judged for not doing something perfectly, ask yourself whether you're actually going to be judged or whether it is just a worry? And if somebody is going to judge you for not doing something perfectly, does that say more about you or more about them? When you're having negative thoughts, reframe your thinking and think about something positive from your day instead. Remember, every day might not be good, but there is something good in every day.

- Increase your self-esteem: When we have a higher self-esteem, we have more confidence in ourselves to make better decisions and feel more able to handle mistakes. Build your self-esteem by finding something you enjoy doing and be ok with the fact that you might not be perfect at it! Is there something that you've always wanted to do but you've never been confident enough to try it? Whether it's a new hobby or stepping out of your comfort zone and talking to somebody new to form a new friendship, improving your mood and how you feel about yourself is a great way to recover from your perfectionism.

- Create "good enough" checklists: Instead of obsessing over every detail, create a checklist that celebrates "good enough" achievements. You'll find this is a good way to reduce your perfectionism and keep your sanity!

- Remind yourself that there is humour in imperfection: Remember that time you did something in front of your friends that was a lot less than perfect and they all laughed? Although this might have stirred up some unhealthy core beliefs about yourself, learning to laugh at your mistakes can be an effective antidote to your perfectionist tendencies.

Watching stand-up comedy or reading some funny stories that emphasise the hilarity of our flaws can also be useful. We are only human, after all!

- Start small and be compassionate with yourself: Instead of criticising yourself for your mistakes, view them as opportunities for growth. Acknowledge the effort you put into something instead of the outcome.

- Just do something because "why the hell not?!": Still stuck in analysis paralysis deciding which air fryer to buy? Just take a risk and pick one because why the hell not! I mean, what's the worst that could happen?!

- Regulate your nervous system: When you are feeling anxious about getting something wrong or not doing something perfectly, it is more than likely that your body is in fight or flight mode. We need to regulate our nervous system to get back to a state of balance and calm. This can be achieved through various techniques such as deep breathing, mindfulness or grounding exercises which help to signal to our body that we are safe and that there is no immediate threat.

Overcoming perfectionism isn't easy, but it is a necessary step if we want to feel better about ourselves, and let's be honest, save ourselves some time in life! Imagine how much time you could save if you didn't need to analyse every single detail before making a decision, or if you could just send that email without checking it a ridiculous amount of times! By learning to accept imperfections and flaws, we can begin to see that life can be messy and unpredictable no matter what we do, and this will ultimately help us adjust the unrealistic standards we've imposed upon ourselves.

Top tips for getting over your perfectionist traits:

1. STOP aiming for 100% perfection and aim for progress instead.
2. DO find the humour in imperfection. Laughter is the best medicine, after all!
3. DUMP the need to do everything perfectly all of the time! Some things can just be "good enough!".

CHAPTER 14

I just can't be bothered today

Do you ever have the feeling that you just really can't be arsed? Whether it's getting that boring work task done, folding up that huge pile of washing, or actually getting off your backside and finally exercising like you had promised yourself you would since January 1st when it's now mid-May. We've all been there! Whilst it's completely normal to feel demotivated from time to time, if you find that it is something you struggle with more often than not, it might be time to take a deeper look into this.

If you notice yourself not wanting to get off the sofa and wanting to just sit there with Netflix on in the background whilst endlessly scrolling on TikTok, instead of beating yourself up, be curious about it and check in with yourself. Ask yourself how you are actually feeling. How long have you been doing this (and I don't just mean today, I mean is this a long-term pattern for you)? What is it that's actually stopping you from doing what you need to do? Is there a fear of failure attached to your lack of motivation? Are you beating yourself up for not doing what you said you would do? Are you not motivated to do that exercise because you're thinking "what's the point?"? If you are having negative thoughts surrounding what you need to do, it might be that your core beliefs are having a part to play in how you feel about yourself, which is in turn influencing how you feel about doing what you want or need to do.

If you notice that this lack of motivation is a long-term pattern for you, it might be worth thinking about your childhood and your inner child. If you experienced trauma in your childhood, be it physical or emotional, you probably grew up living in survival mode and were most likely on high alert for any threats. You might have felt as though if you relaxed, something bad would happen. For example, you might have been constantly on high alert if your parent or caregiver shouted at you for watching TV when they wanted you to be doing something more productive. If as a child you were never allowed to have lazy days, lie in at the weekends, or perhaps made to feel as though taking breaks or relaxing was "lazy", it might be that your rebellious inner child is coming to the forefront and taking over. Was there a particular time or incident in your younger years where perhaps you were scolded for being "lazy" or weren't allowed to do something you wanted to do. Think about how old you were at this time. Picture what you looked like. What was going on in your life at this time? Did you feel as though you just needed a break in some way, but it just wasn't allowed to happen? Do you remember a time when you just needed to retreat into yourself and hide away? If you can relate to any of these scenarios, it might be that your inner child might be saying "I can do what I want now!". In the midst of the lack of motivation might be a sense of empowerment, that you are actually CHOOSING this, and maybe that wasn't an option for you in your childhood. However, this might now be resulting in your adult self lying around and neglecting the things you know you should be doing.

If this is something that resonates with you, remind yourself that it's all very well and good being in control of your life and not having to answer to anyone, but if you notice that you often feel demotivated, it might begin to have a detrimental effect on your life. If you can't be bothered to cook, you're probably not going to eat as healthily as you could, which will most likely make you feel like crap. If you can't be bothered to get on top of the boring household tasks you need to do, they're just going to keep building up until you can't see your kitchen worktop because there are so many dirty dishes on it, which is probably going to make you feel like crap. And if you don't get that work task done by the time your boss wants it done, well, there might be repercussions for this as well, which will probably make you feel like…yeah you've guessed it, crap! So, we really need a way to get out of this cycle of low mood and motivation and get into a better cycle!

One way to do this is to use the journalling technique to get in touch with that younger part of you who wants to sit on the sofa watching Netflix. Try to channel the younger version of you and see what they have to say. You might be surprised by what comes out. There might be a hurt, angry, younger self deep down who has had enough of being told what to do and wants to make their own choices, whether they are good or bad. This exercise might make you feel emotional, but that's not always a bad thing. If you feel emotional, it means that you are getting to the route of the problem. Once you have written the journal entry from the point of your view of your younger self, it's then time to write one back from your adult self. If your inner child felt angry at your parent for ignoring you, not spending enough time with you, not understanding you, or whatever the issue might have been, now is the time to tell your younger self what you needed to hear at the time. If you were sitting next to your younger self at the time, what would you say to them? Would you tell them that you will always be here for them and that they will always have you to turn to? Would you tell them that they are safe now? Tell them from your adult perspective what you needed to hear at the time, and watch how your emotions start to shift.

Hopefully connecting with your inner child might help you get to the root of the problem, but if you want some quick-fire strategies for when you just really can't be arsed, then look no further!

- Have you ever had the thought "I'll do x/y/x when I have more energy" or "I'll do x/y/z when my mood is better", or "I'll go to that new exercise class when I feel more confident"? I'm sure we can all relate to a time like this, and what we are doing here is waiting for either the emotion or a physical sensation to change before we do something. The only problem with this is, quite a lot of the time, the action actually comes before the emotion. So, if you're waiting around to suddenly feel like you really can't wait to do that huge pile of washing, I'm sorry to tell you but you might be waiting a while! Whereas if we actually push ourselves to do something even if we don't want to, it usually gives us a bit more energy and motivation to continue, and actually improves our mood because we are getting a sense of achievement. Although we might think we need to feel something good in order to do something, this isn't usually the case, and quite a lot of the time we just need to push ourselves at the start to get the motivation we need to continue. So, stop waiting and start doing!

- In addition to the point above, one way to trick your brain into doing something you just can't be bothered to do is to tell yourself you'll just do it for ten minutes. For example, if you really don't want to do the washing up or tidy your wardrobe like you've been telling yourself you'll do for weeks, tell yourself that you'll do it but only for ten minutes. This has two purposes. Firstly, usually if we begin doing something, we get into it and then get a sense of motivation which makes us want to continue beyond the ten minutes. So, you might start tidying your wardrobe and then be pleasantly surprised when you finish it and move on to the next task! The second purpose of this is, even if you do only do ten minutes of the task, you have actually done what you set out to do, which should give you a sense of achievement. If we set ourselves unrealistic expectations that are too high, we are only going to feel miserable when we don't achieve them. So, start small, and build up from there.

- Do something physical to boost your energy levels! Go for a brisk walk around the block (yes, even if it's cold!) or do 20 star jumps on the spot! Or put your headphones in, turn the volume up and dance around the kitchen to your favourite song!

- Make sure you plan a reward for yourself for when you've done whatever it is you don't want to do. Treat yourself with your favourite chocolate bar, call a friend or watch the next episode on your latest series. It doesn't have to be a huge reward, but by giving yourself something you see as positive and enjoy doing, you will help rewire your brain into doing the things you don't want to do.

- Look better, feel better. If you're slobbing around in your pjs and haven't washed your hair in days, you probably aren't going to feel great either, which is only going to impact your mood and motivation levels. I'm not saying put on a ballgown to do the housework (but hey, if it works for you then why not!), but self-care does go a long way in terms of how it impacts our mood. If you're feeling low, get in the shower, wash your hair, get dressed in clothes you would actually leave the house in, and see how much better you feel. Basically, what I'm saying is, if you're feeling low, add lipstick and attack!

- Make a plan and write it down! How many times have you told yourself you'll do this or that tomorrow or next week, and tomorrow or next week comes and you still haven't done it? I can't even count the amount of times I've said I'll do something tomorrow and just haven't got around to it. But if we actually put pen to paper (or thumbs to phone screens!) and add it to our diary, we are more likely to follow through with it and not forget about it.

- Determine what works for you when you feel like this. If you try some of these strategies, don't expect them all to work for you the first time you do them. Everyone is different, and what works for one person might not necessarily work for another. When you know what works for you, use it!

- And lastly, be compassionate with yourself. Telling yourself how lazy you are isn't going to get anything done, and it's not going to make you feel better. Be kind to yourself, and talk to yourself like you would a friend.

Feeling demotivated and low in energy is common for all of us at times, but for some of us it can be rooted in unresolved childhood trauma or emotional unmet needs. Being able to recognise these feelings as signals rather than failures allows us to approach ourselves with compassion. Small actions can gradually restore our energy. By nurturing our inner child and addressing our past wounds, we can create a foundation for renewed motivation and energy so we can put a stop to the doom scrolling and actually do something productive!

Top tips to get rid of the "I can't be arsed" and get some motivation!

1. STOP being hard on yourself, it won't change anything!
2. DO connect with your inner child to look more deeply into whether there is a reason you get stuck in this freeze response. Journalling or visualisation techniques will help with this.
3. DUMP the negative thoughts you have about yourself in that moment, and focus on something positive that will increase your productivity!

CHAPTER 15

Me? Overthinking? Only on the days that end in y...

I'm sure we can all say without a doubt that there has definitely been a time in our life when we have become caught up in massively overthinking a situation.

Who are we kidding?

There have been so many of those times we probably can't even count them! Did we say the wrong thing to our new boss? Did they catch us stumbling on our words on that Teams call and now think we can't do the job? Did Jane at work see the coffee stain on your blouse that you desperately tried to wash and dry under the hand dryer in the toilets? Or perhaps you said something unintentionally insensitive to Doris at number 62 after her beloved cat went missing? Whatever it is, we've all been in the situation where we've thought, "shit, what have I done".

Even though we've all been in this situation, it becomes a problem when our overthinking becomes all-consuming, and we can't control our worries. Overthinking is a maladaptive coping mechanism; it makes us feel better in the short term as we feel as though we have some control over the situation, but worse in the long term as we spend so much time thinking about negative outcomes.

We might notice that we worry about every little thing and think "what if" in every situation. When we think about our worries, we can generally divide them into two categories. Firstly, we have our practical worries – these are worries about a current situation in the here and now, which we have some control over. For example, "my car has broken down on the motorway" is a practical worry as it's a present situation which we are able to problem solve. Secondly, we have our "what if" worries, which are hypothetical worries, they are future based, and we don't have any control over them. An example of a "what if" worry would be "what if it rains next weekend and I have to cancel my barbecue". It's a worry based in the future, and ultimately, we don't have any control over it.

If we look back at our practical worry of our car breaking down on the motorway, we do have some control over this. We can problem solve this by considering all of the options available to us in this situation; we can call the RAC, or our brother's mechanic friend who has got us out of some less than desirable situations with our car before. Whatever we do, we have options, and we won't be stranded on the motorway in two days' time. However, there comes a problem when we try and solve our "what if" worries in the same way as we solve our practical ones. Our brains are problem solving machines, and they are constantly trying to solve problems and find the answers to situations. This is great when it comes to our practical worries, as these need resolving; however, it is less helpful when it comes to our hypothetical worries, as our brain will try to find a solution as it does with our practical worries, but what it doesn't understand is that this worry hasn't happened and it is future based, therefore an exact solution isn't possible. Therefore, our brains will run through 100 (sometimes 1000, but who's counting!) different solutions for each eventuality, but there won't ever be a definite answer. If we take the example of "what if it rains next weekend and I have to cancel my barbecue", we could consider the options of postponing it, eating inside instead, or getting a gazebo. We might spend hours or days worrying about it and considering every option, but ultimately, we don't have any control over whether or not it rains.

When it comes to our hypothetical worries, we have a habit of jumping to the worst case scenario very quickly, without pausing to consider any other possibilities. But if we were to stop and think, ask yourself, how many of your "what if" worries have actually happened? If you were to look at them over the past two weeks, two months, two years, or even your whole life, on a scale of 0-100% where would you put the hypothetical worries that have actually materialised? Would it really be 100%? It might seem like it at times, but when you think about it rationally, do ALL of your worst case scenario "what if" worries actually happen? Or is it only a minimal amount of them? Next time you notice yourself getting caught up in overthinking the worst possible case scenario and worrying incessantly about it, ask yourself how often your "what if" worries actually happen.

Our "what if" worries always transport us into the future in an invisible time machine. Think about it: when we worry, we are in the future as we are predicting a negative outcome. We can't worry about the past, as it has already happened. We might feel depressed, upset, or angry about the past, we can dwell on it and ruminate over negative events, but we don't worry about them, as we already know the outcome. The problem with this time machine though, is that the reality it takes us to quite often doesn't exist. When we think about all of our worries that haven't happened, we realise that all of those sleepless nights were, quite honestly, a waste of time, as everything turned out fine. And the times it didn't turn out how we wanted it to, we still got through it. When you notice that your mind has taken you to a future reality, just stop, take a breath, and acknowledge those worries. Then remind yourself, "this is a future based worry, I don't have any control over this right now" and bring your focus of attention back to the present. Ask yourself what you are doing in this moment that you do have control over. Were you working when you noticed your mind wandering? Can you bring your attention back to the present and really focus on your work and put 100% effort into it? If you were watching TV when your mind started taking you to the worst case scenario, can you refocus on what you were watching and give it all of your attention?

Another way to bring your attention back to the here and now is by using something called grounding techniques. This is where you ground yourself in the present moment using your five senses.

Try and find:

- Five things you can see around you (it can be anything!) in your immediate surroundings. If it gets a bit boring just naming five things you can see, you can make it a little more interesting by naming five objects of a particular colour, or five objects which are a particular shape, or five objects beginning with a certain letter. This takes us a bit longer and takes our attention away from our anxiety for a longer period of time. And sometimes it can be quite fun! It's like the adults' I spy!

- Four things you can hear. It could be traffic you can hear outside your window, the clock ticking, or the humming of your laptop as you work.

- Three things you can feel. This can be placing your hands on a surface in front of you and really thinking about what it feels like. Does it feel hard, soft, rough, smooth, warm, cold? It could be feeling the solid floor underneath your feet or the texture of your clothing against your skin. It could also be something you intentionally carry around with you; perhaps a stress ball you can squeeze when you notice your anxious thoughts beginning to creep in, or maybe a shell from the beach that you like the texture of.

- Two things you can smell. This can be naming two smells around you, perhaps that cup of coffee you keep meaning to make, or that new handwash you've just bought for the bathroom. It could even be spraying your favourite perfume on yourself and slowly breathing it in to bring your attention back to the here and now.

- One thing you can taste. This could be taking a sip of drink and really focussing on the taste, or a strong mint that really jolts your taste buds.

When our attention is in the here and now, we feel more at peace as we are more in control and not constantly battling with the "what ifs" of the future. We're more present with those around us and in what we are doing.

When we are worried about the future, we generally underestimate our ability to cope with anything negative. Let's think about it. If someone told you that something bad is going happen to you in two years, and that you will find it really difficult, it will be a really bad time for you and you will struggle to cope, you probably wouldn't stop worrying about it. You'd have endless sleepless nights and it would consume your every thought. However, if someone told you that yes, something will happen to you in two years, it will be a difficult time in your life, BUT, you will get through it and you will absolutely cope with it, your reaction would probably be different. But why? It would be the same situation. The difference is your ability to cope. If we believe we are able to cope with something, we don't have as much need to worry about it, because we know we can handle it.

One of the most important things to remember about life, is that we can't control the situation around us or other people, but we can control how we respond to the situation or other people. Something I often hear from my clients is, "but if I do or say x/y/z, what will people think of me?". It seems to be a lifelong worry that stops people from doing things they want to do. What will your friends or family think if you start dating someone you know they wouldn't approve of? Or what would they think if you ended a relationship with someone they think is perfect for you, but deep down you know they aren't? What will your work colleagues think of you if you don't get that promotion, will they think you're a failure? But then again, what will they think if you do get that promotion? Will they think that now you will look down on them?

And then we have people we don't even know that well. What will that person at the gym think of you if you don't know how to work the new treadmill and you look like you're faffing around? What will the checkout operator at Asda think of you if your card gets declined, even though you know there is money in your account? What will the school mums think of you if your child gets picked up by a childminder whilst you're working full time? The list of worries we can construct in our own minds is never ending!

There is a saying, that what other people think of you is nothing to do with you. And this is so true! No matter how much we might want to control what other people think of us, or their perception of us, we are never going to be able to. People will always think what they are going to think, and we should let them. It's natural to want to feel liked and respected, but wanting to be liked and caring about what other people think about you becomes a problem when you are consumed by worries that begin to affect your everyday life, and when those worries start to impact decisions you make.

We can often trace the need for validation back to our inner child. Do you remember a time when you were at school when you said something that was laughed at by your peers? You may have felt humiliated and vowed never to speak up again. While that experience might have felt monumental at the time, it's likely that your classmates have long forgotten it. In reality, people are too focussed on what is going on in their own lives to give that much thought about our small mistakes. When we think about it rationally, it is very unlikely that somebody is lying awake at night thinking about something that you said years ago. And if they are, it probably says more about them than it does about you! If you can remember a time in your childhood when you were impacted by what somebody thought of you or something somebody said to you, it might be helpful to connect with your inner child and find out how that made her feel at that time. Ask her what she needed at that time and give her some support and validation.

If you grew up without a secure attachment to your main caregiver and did not get a great deal of emotional support, it's likely that you will suffer a low self-esteem and might be more affected by the opinions of other people. Seeking validation can lead to a cycle of people-pleasing behaviour. When you crave the approval of others, it's no surprise you actively try and do things that make other people like you, but at what cost? Preoccupying ourselves with how others perceive us can lead us into a downward spiral of insecurity.

You might notice you care excessively about others' opinions if you find yourself:

- making decisions based upon what you think other people will think of you.
- struggling to maintain personal boundaries.
- finding it difficult to say no, even when you want to.
- hesitating to share your opinion when it differs from those around you.

The more people you meet in your life, the more you will realise how differently everyone thinks, and when you realise how differently everyone thinks, you'll realise that it's impossible to please all of the people all of the time. Take this as an example. You get a new dress to wear on a night out with work colleagues. The colours might be a bit brighter than they are used to seeing you in, it might be a bit shorter than what they are used to seeing you in, so you feel a bit apprehensive about it, because you're already thinking "what will they think?". Let's say that on this night out, three of your work colleagues compliment you on your new dress and tell you how amazing you look in it. Naturally, you feel really good about yourself, it gives you a boost and you're glad you took the risk and wore it, and you will definitely wear it again! However, then let's say a little while later, you overhear a different three work colleagues saying that they think your dress is a bit too loud and a bit too short and they're not sure about it. So now we have a tie. Three people have complimented you on your new dress, and three people aren't sure about it. Now what? Do you a) take on the opinions of the first three colleagues and still feel confident in your decision and wear it again? Or, do you b) listen to the opinions of the other three colleagues which really stick with you, you now feel silly for wearing it and you vow to list it on Vinted as soon as you get home? Is there another option to this scenario? Of course, there is always an option c! And option c is, WEAR WHAT YOU

WANT TO WEAR REGARDLESS OF OTHER PEOPLE'S OPINIONS! If somebody likes what you're wearing, that's great; if they don't, that's fine too, it really isn't any of their business.

Instead of trying to control what other people think of us, we should be trying to control our own thoughts. After all, these are the only ones we have control over, and if we spend our time focussing on our own growth and self-development, we are less likely to be fazed by the opinions of other people, because, let's face it, we just don't have the time for that!

One thing I love to hear from my clients is how their lives would look if they were less concerned about what other people thought of them. Think about it, and REALLY let yourself reflect on this question. If we had a magic wand, and we could wave away the fear of other people's opinions, what would your life look like? What would be different about it? Would you wear something you've always wanted to wear but have never had the courage? Would you be in the same relationship? If you're single, would you be with somebody you want to be with, but are too scared because of the judgement from others around you? Would you be more open and share your opinions more, without the fear of being criticised? Would you tell somebody NO for once in your life rather than trying to please everybody? Would you stand up for yourself to that family member who you know deep down you need to put your foot down with? If we were to really give this question some thought, we could all most likely find one thing in our lives that would be different if we weren't as concerned about what somebody thought about us. So, ask yourself what is stopping you from taking back control of your life, and living it the way you want to live it. Once you have found the answer to that question, it might be time to start setting some boundaries (see chapter on boundaries!) and begin living your life your way! Remember, the people who mind don't matter, and the people who matter don't mind!

Another way to alleviate your thoughts about what other people think of you is to limit your exposure to negative influences. Look at the relationships you have with the people around you. Try and surround yourself with people who are supportive and encourage you. Reducing your contact with critical or judgemental people can help you feel more secure in expressing yourself.

It can also be helpful to focus on action instead of thoughts. Instead of ruminating on what others might think, shift your energy toward taking action on things that are important to you. This will help to redirect your thoughts and build confidence in your choices.

Finally, it can be helpful to limit your social media consumption (yes, I did say that!). Consider reducing your time on social media where comparisons and judgements are right in front of your face. Try and find something more meaningful to do with your time which won't lead to you comparing your life to other people's and worrying about what they think of yours.

Overall, let's remember that the opinions of others are just that – opinions. They don't define who we are or dictate our worth; and spending time worrying about what other people think of us is draining and upsetting to US – it doesn't actually impact them! So next time you find yourself stuck in a negative thought spiral about what Becky at work really thinks about you, remind yourself that it really doesn't matter. The only person's opinion of yourself that you should really care about is your own.

We all worry at times, and we all let our minds wander to places we don't want them to go. However, looking back at our younger self and understanding where these patterns came from, and breaking our worries down into practical and hypothetical worries can really help us break the cycle of overthinking. Instead of allowing our thoughts to spiral, we can use grounding techniques and self-compassion that will ultimately help us build more resilience when it comes to managing our worries. The most important thing to remember when managing our overthinking is to bring ourselves back to the present and remind ourselves that the future might not be as bad as we think it will be!

Top tips for reducing worrying and caring less about what other people think of you:

1. STOP making decisions based on what other people think of you. Make decisions based on your own opinions and what is important to you.

2. DO get in touch with your inner child and think about that early memory of someone thinking negatively of you. Ask yourself what it was you needed at that time. Kindness? Compassion? Practise giving whatever it is you needed back then to yourself now.

3. And finally, DUMP the thought that you won't be able to cope if something bad happens in your life. You are stronger than you think, you've got this!

CHAPTER 16
Building Resilience

E motional resilience is a bit more than bouncing back from Dave like a pro! We all face hard times in life, breakups, work stress, and occasionally stepping on Lego bricks with bare feet (that's definitely the worst one!), but the secret is how you respond to these situations. The more resilient you become, the quicker you can turn a crappy day into a moment of growth. The less resilient you are, the more likely you are to wallow in a pity party for one and get sucked into a spiral of misery and despair. Sound familiar? Keep reading!

Emotional resilience is basically our ability to overcome the crap that goes on in our lives. It involves the capacity to manage our emotions, maintain a positive outlook (hard sometimes, I know!), and navigate these difficulties whilst minimising your distress levels. Some key aspects of emotional resilience include:

- Self-awareness: Understanding your emotions and recognising how they impact your thoughts and behaviours.
- Emotional regulation: The ability to control emotional responses and manage stress effectively.
- Problem-solving skills: Developing strategies to confront and overcome challenges.
- Social support: Utilising relationships and support networks to cope with difficulties.

- Optimism: Maintaining hope and a positive outlook and believing in your ability to overcome difficulties.
- Flexibility: Being open to change and willing to adjust to new circumstances (even when you don't want to!).

First of all, let's consider what contributes to our emotional resilience. Usually it's a combination of genetics, environmental factors and (surprise!) our childhood experiences. The way we learned to handle emotions as a child has a huge impact on how we cope with adult stress. As our inner child is a filing cabinet of everything we have ever experienced, from the highs of winning that spelling test to the gut-wrenching lows of your best friend at five years old no longer wanting to be your best friend, it makes sense that when we face adult challenges, for example job loss or relationship issues, the response of our inner child often emerges first. Those who have experienced trauma in their childhood may find it more difficult to develop emotional resilience due to:

- Having a low self-esteem: Trauma can instil a sense of worthlessness, making it challenging for childhood trauma survivors to believe in their ability to overcome difficulties.
- Fear of vulnerability: People with childhood trauma may build protective barriers around their emotions which limit their ability to express themselves and seek help.
- Difficulty with relationships: Past trauma can lead to trust issues, making it hard to develop supportive connections that boost resilience.
- Persistent negative emotions: Childhood trauma survivors often struggle with anxiety, depression and anger, which can cloud their ability to process emotions and recover from setbacks.

If you can relate to any of the above, don't worry! Despite these challenges, it is possible to build emotional resilience, even if you have been affected by childhood trauma.

Building resilience can be a unique journey for everyone that takes time and effort, and it can be more difficult when you have grown up in a chaotic environment and have negative core beliefs about yourself. But it is by no means impossible.

There are many things we can do to help build our emotional resilience:

Acknowledge your feelings: The first step in building emotional resilience is acknowledging the impact of your childhood trauma. This involves understanding the inner child's feelings and recognising how our past experiences can shape our present behaviour. A lot of self-reflection and journalling can help with this!

Connect with your inner child: Engage with your inner child to enable them to feel heard and heal your past wounds. You can do this by using visualisation techniques, journalling, or getting creative and using play strategies. Some journalling questions you may want to ask yourself to help build your emotional resilience are:

1. What childhood experiences have I noticed that impacted my ability to feel secure and resilient?
2. How did I typically cope with difficult emotions growing up?
3. Are there any recurring patterns in my emotional responses that might stem from childhood experiences?
4. What messages did I receive about my emotions when I was a child?
5. In what ways can I show compassion and understanding towards my inner child?

6. How do I currently respond to stress or adversity? How might my childhood experiences have influenced these responses?

7. What protective factors from my childhood helped me feel safe and supported? How can I incorporate these into my adult life?

8. What are some healthy ways I can nurture my emotional wellbeing today?

9. Reflect on a recent challenging situation. How did I handle it, and what could I do differently to build resilience?

10. What self-care practices can I develop to strengthen my emotional resilience?

11. Are there any unresolved childhood wounds that still affect my emotional stability? How can I begin to address them?

12. How can I set healthy boundaries to protect my emotional wellbeing?

13. What strengths and qualities have helped me bounce back from setbacks so far?

14. How does reconnecting with my inner child empower me in facing adult challenges?

15. What steps can I take to create a supportive environment for my emotional growth?

By answering these questions, you are going to be able to really reflect on your resilience levels and the steps you can take to improve them.

Develop problem solving skills: Although it would be great if life was always plain sailing (albeit a little boring, don't you think?!), there are always going to be times when something rocks the boat. This is when we need problem solving skills! If you accidentally burn the dinner you've been looking forward to all day (yes I've done this too many times!), why bother standing there f-ing and blinding and thinking "what's the point, I'll just go hungry!". Although we've probably all thrown our toys out of the pram when something has gone wrong at one time or another in our lives, it doesn't get us anywhere and certainly doesn't solve any problems. So next time you burn your dinner, problem solve with a back-up plan! Do you have a microwave meal somewhere? Can you make a meal out of the little ingredients you have before your food shop arrives tomorrow? Be creative! Your inner child will appreciate the improvisation.

Mindfulness and presence: Take some time to unplug from the chaos! Mindfulness is crucial in building resilience. Spend five minutes meditating or simply breathing deeply. You're not going to gain any emotional resilience running around like a headless chicken every time something goes wrong, so get zen and get in touch with your inner peace.

Build supportive relationships: This isn't just about having friends to call every time Dave pisses you off (but yes that is definitely a plus!). Surround yourself with supportive people who get you and who you feel comfortable to go to when you need help and support. We all have those people in our lives who drain our energy and take more than they give (you already know who I'm talking about as you're reading this!). Those people aren't going to help you build any emotional resilience. Make sure you are spending your time with positive people and take a step back from anyone who is making you feel stressed and drained.

Establish healthy boundaries: Learning to set and maintain healthy boundaries is essential for building emotional resilience. This includes knowing when to say no, protecting your time and energy, ensuring your relationships are reciprocal and supportive instead of being Dave's doormat!

Practise self-compassion: Being more compassionate with ourselves allows us to treat ourselves with kindness and understanding rather than criticism. This can alleviate feelings of shame or guilt associated with past experiences, making it easier to build resilience.

Take small risks: Start saying "yes" to things and learn to tolerate the uncertainty that comes with it. The more you are able to tolerate uncertainty, the more resilient you will become as you will learn that you ARE able to cope with challenges.

Get physical!: Regular physical activity is a powerful tool for building resilience. Exercise releases endorphins which can help improve mood and relieve stress. Remember that time you felt like you were going to die during that run or on the treadmill? But you didn't. You did it and you felt a hell of a lot better for it after! So next time you feel as though you can't face whatever problem you've got going on in your life, do some exercise and get your blood flowing and see how much more capable you feel after!

Life is always going to throw us curveballs sometimes, that is the nature of being human. The key isn't avoiding these difficulties, but rather gaining the strength to navigate through them. Emotional resilience is about recognising our inner capacity to recover, grow and even transform ourselves when we face problems or adversity. Remember, it's ok to fall as long as you get back up again, because ultimately, resilient people aren't people who never stumble, they are those who refuse to stay down for too long. And if you're having a bad day and need to improve your emotional resilience, listen to a song called Tubthumping by Chumbawamba (a 90s song for any of you who are too young to have a clue what I'm going on about!). Once you listen to the chorus, you'll have a new outlook on whatever it is going on in your life!

Top tips to improve your emotional resilience:

1. STOP wallowing in self-pity and thinking you can't solve problems. You have totally got the ability to cope with whatever you've got going on right now, you just need to believe it!

2. DO start taking small risks and tolerating the uncertainty that comes with them. Know that you can manage the outcome, no matter what happens.

3. DUMP any relationships that bring you down and only put your time and effort into people who get you and help build your emotional resilience instead of tearing it down (you know who those people are!).

CHAPTER 17
Self- Esteem

Self-esteem is the term used to describe how we think and feel about ourselves and our achievements. Although it sounds the same as self-worth, is is different as our self-esteem refers to the way we evaluate our abilities, qualities and overall value based on our beliefs about ourselves, whereas self-worth is a deeper more intrinsic sense of value which is unconditional and not dependent on external achievements or approval. Self-esteem is basically our opinions of ourselves. If you have a high self-esteem you are likely to value yourself, your life and the things you have achieved. However, if you have a low self-esteem, you aren't likely to value yourself and probably minimise your achievements. Although it is common to feel crap about ourselves and lack confidence from time to time (I'm sure we can all relate to a time when we felt not so great about ourselves), if you feel like this more often than not, it is likely that you have a low self-esteem. Having a low self-esteem can drastically impact the quality of our lives, as it can be a driver for negative thoughts and lead us down the path of avoidance which inevitably leads to becoming stuck in unhealthy patterns.

So what causes a low self-esteem? Well I'm sure you can already guess, but it goes back to our childhood, again! Low self-esteem can be caused by trauma experienced in our childhood, for example abandonment by a parental figure, abuse, neglect or being punished. It can also be caused by our parents or caregivers being highly critical and having overly high expectations of us and being made to feel as though we don't meet their high standards, for example being criticised for "only" getting a certain score on a test. It can also be caused by experiences outside of the home, for example being bullied at school or always feeling like you were the "odd one out". In addition, low self-esteem might develop if we grew up feeling alone and if we didn't feel as though we had anyone to talk to about how we were feeling or provide us with emotional support or validation.

Having said that, low self-esteem doesn't always develop from things that are said or done to us as children, it can also develop when things are not said. For example, if you grew up with parents or caregivers who never told you that you were loved, capable or special, you are unlikely to grow up feeling these things about yourself. Perhaps you weren't praised for your achievements or maybe they were taken for granted and not talked about, leaving you with a sense of inadequacy or failure.

A low self-esteem is associated with negative core beliefs we hold about ourselves which we developed in our childhood (go back to the chapter on core beliefs if you need a refresher!). If there was a situation you remember when you were younger which caused you to feel a high level of emotion, it is likely that some core beliefs were formed from this. For example, maybe you remember a time when you were so excited to tell your parents about something you did well at school, only for it to be brushed over as though it wasn't that important, or if you lived in the shadow of a more academic sibling, it is likely that this would have caused you to feel inadequate as a child. When a situation arises as an adult that evokes the same emotions as this time, for example feeling as though your boss always favours your work colleague and their achievements over you and your achievements, we then act in line with the beliefs that have already been created. For example, if you have the belief "I'm inadequate" or "I'm a failure", you're less likely to apply for a promotion or make the jump to apply for a new job you really want because you already don't believe you are capable of getting it, so you end up thinking "what's the point" and not applying. Equally, if you have the belief of "I'm inadequate", you might feel too anxious to start anything new, so you don't join that new gym class you've been wanting to try for ages because you don't want to be rubbish at it and look silly in front of other people.

Our negative core beliefs are kind of like an abusive relationship. They lie to us and tell us that they are keeping us safe and stopping us from experiencing any more emotional distress, when in actual fact they are holding us prisoner in our comfort zone, making us too scared to step outside it. As we have already talked about, past experiences from our childhood leave an imprint on us as adults, making us doubt our capabilities and exacerbating our failures. Even though you might be successful, you may still feel insecure. If you have a critical inner voice telling you that your achievements aren't good enough or that you aren't good enough, ask yourself where this critical voice comes from. Is it yours? Or is it a critical parent or caregiver? It's more than likely that this critical voice comes from your younger years and is a constant reminder that what you're doing isn't good enough, or worse, YOU aren't good enough. The problem with this critical inner voice (well, there are many problems with it, but this is a big one!) is that it becomes a self-fulfilling prophecy, meaning that if you keep listening to it telling you that you're not good enough, you will miss opportunities because you won't believe that you are worthy of them, which perpetuates your low self-esteem.

Our self-esteem can have a detrimental impact on our relationships as adults. If we have negative core beliefs about ourselves, we are likely to believe that we aren't good enough, aren't loveable or aren't worthy, meaning that we're likely to attract the same relationships with people who always let us down or don't treat us how we deserve to be treated. If we didn't receive love or affection as a child, we will likely find it wherever we can, even if we know deep down that that person isn't treating us well. We might also engage in our own negative behaviours in a relationship, such as withdrawing our love as a punishment, trying to make somebody jealous, or being clingy and needy and requiring constant validation and reassurance. This is because your inner child is wounded, and if your needs weren't met in your childhood, you are going to constantly search for them to be met as an adult, whatever the cost. But by healing those wounds and improving our self-esteem, we will be able to feel more secure in our relationships, and not tolerate anything less than we deserve, so any Daves that aren't treating us right can be kicked to the kerb without a second thought.

So how do we improve our self-esteem?

First of all, acknowledge the existence of your inner child: Are there any particular times in your life which you can pinpoint that may have led you to develop a low self-esteem? Did you have a critical parent who made you feel as though nothing you did as a child (or an adult) was/is good enough? Did you feel as though you needed to earn their love and approval? As we've talked about previously, you can use visualisation or journalling techniques to connect with your inner child and strike up a conversation with them. Ask them how they are feeling and provide them with some comfort, reassurance and understanding. Pay attention to any feelings of happiness or sadness which might arise whilst you are doing this and make space to acknowledge and sit with those emotions.

Reparent yourself: Think about how you would treat a child who is scared or hurting, and offer yourself the same level of compassion and care. This might involve self-soothing practices such as deep breathing, mindfulness or creating a safe space for relaxation. You could even make some time for activities that you enjoyed as a child, whether that's drawing, playing or spending time in nature.

Challenge your negative self-talk: Become aware of the internal dialogues you have with yourself. When negative thoughts arise, counter them with affirmations or positive reinforcements. For example, instead of telling yourself that you're not good enough, use another statement such as "I am good enough just as I am". Think about compliments you have received in the past. Although these might not be at the forefront of your mind (we always tend to forget the positive things people say to us and remember anything negative!), you will have received them at some point in your life. If you can remember some specific examples of compliments or a time someone has said something kind to you, write them down in a journal and read them on a regular basis. One exercise I like to do with my clients is to ask them to ask people close to them to write down three things about them, not telling them whether to write positive or negative things. People are usually surprised at what others have to say about them!

Set boundaries: A big part of loving yourself is establishing boundaries. This involves saying NO to situations or people that drain your energy or make you feel unworthy (bye Dave!). Boundaries protect our emotional wellbeing and make sure that we don't become a chronic people-pleaser and put our needs at the back of the queue!

Self-care: It might sound so clichéd, but self-care isn't a luxury, it's a necessity! Create a self-care routine that incorporates your physical, emotional and mental wellbeing. This might include going to bed early, eating healthily, staying hydrated, exercising, maintaining positive friendships, setting goals and just generally engaging in activities that you enjoy!

Work on your emotional resilience: Improving your emotional resilience will really help with your self-esteem! Learn to take risks and tolerate the uncertainty that comes with it. Say YES to opportunities you wouldn't usually say yes to, whether it's starting a new hobby or eating at a restaurant you've never eaten at before! Saying yes to things will begin to open up your world and get out of that cycle of avoidance!

Learn to take compliments: Next time someone tells you how good you look in that new top, or how much they appreciated you helping them understand the new IT system at work, instead of brushing it off and saying "oh no I don't" or "it was nothing", accept the compliment and add it to your journal!

Celebrate small wins: Acknowledge and celebrate your achievements, no matter how small they seem. This helps to create a sense of accomplishment and reinforces your self-worth as well as your self-esteem.

Building a healthy self-esteem is a journey of reconnecting with our inner child, healing past wounds and embracing our true worth. Our childhood experiences shape how we view ourselves, but they don't have to define us permanently. By practising self-care, challenging our negative beliefs and finally setting some bloody boundaries (yes, I'm talking about Dave!) we can create a balanced and resilient self-esteem.

Top tips to improve your self-esteem:

1. STOP listening to that critical inner voice when it tells you that you aren't good enough and connect with your inner child to give them some words of comfort and support.

2. DO accept compliments and celebrate your achievements. You would celebrate your friend's achievements so now is the time to start celebrating your own!
3. DUMP the negative self-talk and learn to talk to yourself with compassion and kindness! You are worthy of your own love!

CHAPTER 18

Resistance to Change

Let's have a think about something we all encounter, yet sometimes dread: change. If you've noticed that your inner child tends to have a complete meltdown when faced with change in your life, you're definitely not alone! Your inner child wants to feel safe, secure and loved. If you experienced trauma or instability in your childhood, she might whisper (or scream!) for you to cling on tightly to what you know. She sees routines and familiar environments as comforting, but let's be honest, sometimes staying in the same place in life or the same situation can be very constricting.

Think about it. If you had a traumatic experience in your childhood associated with abandonment, if you are later confronted with change in your adult life, this might trigger memories of those feelings of insecurity and fear. Your adult self knows that stepping out of your comfort zone might lead to amazing opportunities, but your younger self is just trying to keep you safe from what feels like the unknown abyss.

Imagine you're in a job that doesn't light you up anymore. You can't wait for Friday afternoon and by Sunday evening you've got that pit in your stomach because you know that when your alarm goes off in the morning, it's time to go back. You really can't stand it anymore, but the thought of leaving and starting afresh scares the living daylights out of you, so you don't do anything to change it. The very essence of change, like changing jobs, ending or beginning a relationship, or even trying out a new hairstyle, can feel like standing at the edge of a cliff whilst being chased by a lion. You know you're going to have to jump into the ocean when it catches up with you, but you're too scared to make the jump any sooner than you have to. Your vulnerable inner child might urge you to stay where you are, even if your adult self knows that at some point, the jump is inevitable.

Resisting change can lead to stagnation in different parts of our lives. Relationships might suffer because you're afraid to express your needs or emotions, or you might end up staying in a relationship you don't want to be in because it feels safer than not being in it. Imagine putting up with Dave's shitty behaviour for the rest of your life because you're too scared to be without him. But ask yourself what it is that you're actually afraid of? Usually we aren't afraid to get rid of the arsehole who's treating us badly; we know that's what we need to do. But it's everything that comes after it.

"What if I don't find anyone else?"

"What if I realise when he's gone that he wasn't that bad? Then I'll realise I made a mistake and he won't take me back."

"What if he was actually the one and I was just overreacting?"

"What if he tells everyone horrible things about me? I wouldn't be able to cope with that. It's probably better to stay with him then I don't have to deal with that."

So then what happens? We end up staying with him longer than we should because we're too scared of all the "what ifs" and the change that comes after it. Your adult self knows what he's like and knows he won't change, but your inner child just wants to stick with what she knows because she's suffered too much trauma already. It's exactly the same with the job situation. You might have thoughts like "but what if I don't find another job?", or "what if I do find another job and I hate it and then I'm stuck there". There is always a "what if" which keeps us stuck in the same situation because we're afraid. Past trauma from our childhood makes us feel vulnerable, and keeps the life we want out of reach because we're too afraid to make the changes we need to make to get there. This battle between safety and change often leaves us feeling stuck and unfulfilled.

So let's just stop and ask the million-dollar question: what's so bad about change anyway? Let's think about it. Change is like a caterpillar's journey to becoming a butterfly. That little caterpillar doesn't know it's destined to spread its colourful wings; it can only feel the discomfort of the cocoon at first. However, once it accepts the process and goes through the transformation, it emerges as a beautiful butterfly, with the ability to fly through the sky; something it definitely couldn't do before entering the cocoon!

Embracing change can lead to exciting new phases in life. Picture your life after Dave. Your new relationship allows you to be your authentic self and you don't need to worry about him taking three to five working days to reply to your last message, or what he's going to say if you see your friends on Friday night instead of him. It might not even be a new relationship that makes you happier, it might be being single and being able to do what you want, when you want, that changes your life for the better. If it's a job you feel stuck in, you might find a career path that fulfills your passions and dreams – doesn't that sound amazing? The trick is allowing yourself to reframe how you view the unknown. Instead of seeing change as something threatening, what if it was framed as an opportunity to grow, learn, and ultimately live your best bloody life?

There is some good news! We can nurture our inner child and make change less scary. Firstly, start by acknowledging your fears and ask yourself what it is you're really afraid of. Was there a time in your childhood where you had a big change that was traumatic? It's completely understandable that you would feel anxious when faced with the prospect of change, especially when you have experienced trauma in the past. Experiencing this as a child usually makes us fear even the smallest changes as an adult. Once you have acknowledged this, take a moment to sit down and have a talk with your inner child. Reassure them that you're here for them, you're in the driver's seat now, and let them know that it's okay to make a change and go into some unfamiliar territory.

Try approaching change with a step by step approach. Start with small alterations in your normal routine. Maybe try a new coffee shop, join a different fitness class, or experiment with a new hobby. As you build confidence in these small changes, your inner child may begin to trust the process and see that you are more than capable of managing these changes. Celebrate these small wins, as they'll help you pave the way for larger changes later on down the line.

Try and see what happens when you view change as an opportunity rather than a threat. Too often when we're faced with change, we think about every little thing that could go wrong or everything that will be bad about it, rather than seeing it as an opportunity. Reflect on the potential benefits of change in a particular situation. What enjoyment, connection, or expertise could come from stepping into the unknown? Keeping a journal can be a powerful tool to record your thoughts and feelings; writing down your dreams and aspirations can provide a roadmap to navigate change with excitement instead of dread! Some journal questions you can ask yourself to help you reflect on your fear of change could be:

1. What specific changes do I find most difficult or uncomfortable to face? Why do I think that is?
2. Can I recall a childhood experience where I felt afraid, unsafe, or powerless in the face of change? How did that experience shape my current feelings about change?

3. In what ways do I tend to resist or avoid change in my life today? What emotions or thoughts come up when I consider making a change?
4. Are there patterns or recurring themes in my resistance to change that might be linked to past trauma or experiences? What are they?
5. How does my body respond when I think about or encounter change? Do I notice physical sensations or emotional reactions?
6. What positive outcomes or benefits might there be in embracing change instead of resisting it? How can I remind myself of these benefits?
7. What supportive strategies or practices can I develop to feel safer and more confident when facing change?
8. How can I nurture my inner child and provide compassion and reassurance during times of transition?
9. Are there specific fears or beliefs I hold about change that I can work on challenging or reframing?
10. What small steps can I take today to gradually become more comfortable with change in my life?

Reflecting on your answers to these questions might help you to get to the root of what it is you don't like about change and shift your perspective on it.

Although our fear of change is usually rooted in the past experiences of our inner child, it doesn't have to dictate our future. Even though change can feel daunting and at times, bloody terrifying, it also holds the potential for our growth and healing. When we begin to view change as an opportunity rather than a threat, we can slowly shift our mindset. Change gives us the chance to rewrite the outcome to our stories in life, rather than living in the same old cycles, and it becomes less intimidating when we approach it with willingness rather than dread. So, if there is a change that deep down you know you need to make, go on and take the jump! Your future self might thank you!

Top tips for dealing with change:

1. STOP avoiding change because you're scared of the unknown. Change can often lead to amazing opportunities in life!
2. DO incorporate a step-by-step approach to change if you're a bit worried about it. Making small changes one step at a time will help to grow your confidence.
3. DUMP the idea that all change is bad; most of the time it won't be as bad as your inner child thinks!

CHAPTER 19

Procrastination – Just five more minutes... right?

Just picture the scene. You're sitting at your desk at work (or at home if you work from home!) and you've got a task list as long as your arm. You've got what feels like 15,000 emails to reply to and Jill from HR is on your back to sign and return that new health and safety policy that is quite frankly as dull as dishwater. You know you need to get started, you need to do something, ANYTHING, but instead you're frozen in procrastination mode. You scroll through your phone, looking at things that really aren't that important to you. You tell yourself you will just scroll for five more minutes, and then it is DEFINITELY time to get some work done. You're already behind, and if you don't start in the next five minutes, there's no way you will catch up by the end of the day. Five minutes passes, and you still don't put your phone down. But it's ok, your boss isn't in the office today, and no one will notice if you're on your phone for another five minutes. Now it's been ten minutes, and you REALLY need to do something. But you need a drink first. That won't take long. And you haven't had a drink all morning, so you really should have one to keep hydrated. You definitely won't be able to work with a headache. You get your drink and get back to your desk. But shouldn't you go to the toilet first? You wouldn't want to start work and really get into the flow of it, and then need to rush off to the toilet. You had better go now, and then you will be able to concentrate properly. Ok so now you've got your drink, been to the toilet, you're back at your desk and ready to begin trawling through that mammoth list of emails. You click onto your front screen, and oh! That looks like an interesting news story. You'll just have a quick read; it won't take long. The one next to it looks interesting too, maybe you'll just have a sneaky look, and then you can really get to work.

You finally finish scrolling through news stories, and somehow find yourself flicking through articles telling you what jumpers to match with which leggings this season – but this is important information, you need to know this! And now that's done, you really need to get to work. You click onto your email inbox, and in the time you've been looking at news stories and fashion tips, you've had another six emails come in. How can that even be possible?! But then you look at the clock, and it's time for lunch in half an hour, so you might be better off just waiting until you've had your lunch, you'll come back nice and refreshed, and then you'll be able to concentrate much better.

Does any of this sound remotely familiar? This, my friend, is known as procrastination, and we are all guilty of it in some way. The word procrastination actually comes from the latin verb "procrastinare", which means to put off until tomorrow (we've all been there!). There are many reasons as to why we procrastinate. Firstly, the idea of completing the task may seem overwhelming, so we try to put it off as long as humanly possible. If it's a work task, perhaps you're not 100% sure on what it is you need to do, but you don't want to ask somebody as you're worried that they might think you're stupid or that you have no idea what you're doing (those childhood beliefs coming back to haunt us again!!). Perhaps there was a time at school when you asked a teacher a question because you didn't understand the work, but instead of getting help you were made to feel as though you should already know the answer, or perhaps you were laughed at by another pupil for asking that question. If there was an experience in your childhood which you feel as though could be connected to you developing negative beliefs about yourself which have led you to procrastinate, you could use the journal technique to connect with your inner child. Some questions you might like to ask yourself are:

- What specific thoughts or feelings come up when I notice myself procrastinating?
- Can I identify any recurring beliefs I have about myself when I face a difficult task? (e.g. I'm a failure, I'm not good enough)
- When did I first start to believe that I am incapable or unworthy? What was happening around that time?
- What messages about myself did I receive from my parents, teachers or caregivers during my childhood?
- How did these messages influence the way I view my abilities and worth today?
- In what ways am I still holding onto childhood fears or beliefs that contribute to my procrastination?
- What emotions do I associate with tasks I tend to put off? (e.g. fear, shame, frustration)
- How do I feel about myself when I delay or avoid certain tasks?
- What would I say to my younger self about the beliefs I hold today?
- What evidence do I have that contradicts my negative beliefs about myself?
- If I imagine completing the task successfully, what core belief needs to change for me to feel comfortable doing it?
- What small steps can I take to challenge and reframe these negative beliefs?

By asking yourself these questions, you will able to get a deeper understanding of what's going on for your inner child when you procrastinate. By connecting with your inner child and asking them what their fear is, you'll be able to give them the reassurance that they need which will help to reframe any negative beliefs.

As well as experiencing a negative event in our childhood which has influenced our beliefs about ourselves and our abilities, there are other reasons we might procrastinate. One reason that we can find ourselves procrastinating is because we tend to view immediate rewards more favourably than future rewards. Of course, we always want to do the pleasurable thing first – why wouldn't we want to do something we enjoy?

Also, let's be completely honest, the thing that you need to do might just be really boring! In this case, you are obviously going to favour doing something that is immediately pleasurable or less boring, rather than doing something that you have absolutely no interest in. However, as we know, there are some things in adult life we need to do, even if we don't want to!

One way to overcome this is to look at yourself through the eyes of your present self and your future self. Your present self might not want the stress of doing this task, you might not want to experience the boredom of doing this task, but your future self will be so pleased you did. If you have a goal you want to achieve, just remember that your future self won't ever achieve it if your present self doesn't get her backside in gear!

We might also procrastinate in order to manage our mood. If we're feeling low that day or particularly anxious, the last thing we want to be doing is that boring task our boss has asked us to do. If something we need to do is boring and doesn't really require us to use any brain power, we can ruminate about whatever it is that's bothering us at the same time, which we know will make us feel worse. On the other hand, if we spend time on our phone, we are more likely to find something that might make us smile and give us that dopamine hit, or at the very least change our focus of attention and give us something else to think about, meaning that our focus of attention isn't on our low mood anymore, it's on whatever we are watching or reading about. For a short period of time, this makes us feel better. But it never lasts!

If we want to manage this form of procrastination, we need to manage our emotions first. What is it that is actually making you feel low or anxious? What emotions or beliefs are you trying to avoid by procrastinating? When you notice yourself in a procrastination cycle, try to remember to be compassionate to yourself. What is the point in noticing yourself not doing the thing you said you would do, and then picking up the stick and hitting yourself with it? Is that really going to change anything? Is being critical towards yourself going to suddenly make you get that task done? No, most probably not, it's more than likely going to make you more annoyed with yourself, which isn't going to do a lot for your mood. And when your mood is low, you're going to do something that makes you feel better, such as…scroll through your phone or watch something on Netflix! So the cycle continues! Instead of criticising yourself, try being compassionate with yourself, and be understanding as to why you're procrastinating. Showing yourself kindness and compassion will decrease your stress levels and increase your feeling of self-worth, making it more likely that you will actually do the task.

If you have perfectionist tendencies, you may procrastinate due to having beliefs about needing to do everything perfectly, or if you can't do something perfectly, you might not see the point in doing it at all. Whilst you are procrastinating, you haven't actually begun the task, meaning that you haven't been able to make a mistake, therefore you haven't had to face any of your negative beliefs about yourself. By not starting the task, it can still be perfect in your head, and delaying it for as long as possible protects you from experiencing any upsetting emotions that might come up if you don't do the task perfectly. However, you probably can't put that task off forever, so instead of avoiding it, it might be helpful to remind yourself that everybody makes mistakes, and that you are NOT a failure if you don't do everything 100% perfectly, you're just human!

Whilst we are in the midst of our procrastination, we are usually aware that whatever we are doing is a bad idea. We know we should put our phone down or that we really need to stop at the end of this episode of the latest Netflix series we're watching. We also know that by continuing to do this, we'll have less time for whatever it is we actually need to be doing, which is inevitably going to lead to us becoming more stressed. But we still continue scrolling or watch the next episode anyway. If you're struggling with procrastination, remind yourself of the positive parts of doing the task. You might not want to do that huge pile of washing up, but you'll feel a sense of achievement when it's done (and you won't have to look at it piled up on the worktop anymore!).

Another way to beat procrastination is to break the task down into more manageable parts. You might have to clean your whole house from top to bottom, but thinking about it like that is only going to make it feel really overwhelming and off-putting. Instead, break it down to one room at a time, and if that seems too much, break the room down into smaller areas and just focus on one area at a time. We are much more likely to begin a task if it feels achievable. If something feels unachievable, we are much less likely to even be bothered to begin in the first place!

Try to identify a time in the day where your energy is higher and you have some free time to do things. It's no good telling yourself you will get that task done in the morning if you're up to your neck in work and childcare. Trying to get things done at an unrealistic time usually leads to us not getting things done at all which then leads us to feeling disappointed and low, which reduces our motivation to get that task done. If you know you have some free time in the evening once work is finished and the kids are in bed, try and get a bit done then. Even if you want to spend the evening relaxing, you'll likely feel much better once it's done, and you can relax properly tomorrow evening without it hanging over you. Alternatively, you might notice you're more of a morning person and are able to get up a bit earlier and get things done first thing so they are out of the way. There isn't a right or wrong, just try different times that work for you, and when you've found that time when you are able to be more productive and feel as though you have a little bit more energy to get those tasks done, stick to it!

You could also try doing the worst task first, just so you know it's out of the way and it isn't hanging over you anymore! It's completely natural to put off the thing you really don't want to do, but if you get that done first, you don't need to worry about it anymore and you've got more headspace to focus on the other tasks you need to achieve. Alternatively, another strategy to manage procrastination is to do your favourite task first, as this is more likely to give you a sense of achievement and energise you, improving your mood ready for the next task.

It can be helpful to plan rewards for yourself after you complete tasks. You might treat yourself to a well-deserved break, in which you can actually do the activities you do when you procrastinate without putting anything off (oh the irony!). Nobody is saying you can't scroll through TikTok or watch Netflix, but maybe there is another time you can do this, and you might even enjoy it more without that nagging voice telling you that you need to do something! Make a list of things you like doing – it might be having a relaxing bath, calling a friend, going for a walk – and make sure you schedule something from the list after you have finished the task. It might even motivate you to get it done!

And finally, try to identify your go-to procrastination activities and excuses. Procrastination activities might be going on your phone, reading a book or magazine, or making sure we've got all the drinks and snacks we need for the task. We might even have some productive procrastination activities, such as tidying up or cleaning. I always tell myself that I can't do anything until everything around me is spotless, but again, I'm just delaying beginning the task I actually need to do due to my own perfectionist tendencies and beliefs. Which, of course, aren't useful! We might even have favourite excuses as to why we are procrastinating (and they seem so believable to us at the time!). It could be that there isn't any point in starting that task now, as it's nearly lunchtime, or it's time for the school run in half an hour, and what would be the point in starting something if you can't finish it right away. The sooner you can identify your most used procrastination activities and excuses, the sooner you can work on challenging them. If your procrastination activity is going on your phone, can you leave your phone in another room whilst you do that task? If it's tidying, instead of tidying everything and putting everything away perfectly, can you make sure that the space you need to do your task in is tidy, and plan to tidy everything else after? (Unless the task you actually need to do is tidying of course!) Once you are able to identify and problem solve your procrastination activities and excuses, you'll be well on your way to building newer, healthier habits!

Procrastination is often a silent cry from our inner child as a way to avoid confronting difficult emotions, fears, or feelings of inadequacy rooted in our childhood experiences. By understanding the emotional roots behind our procrastination and identifying the reason that we are procrastinating, we empower ourselves to make the necessary changes we need to make to help us to get things done. Remember, change is a gradual process, so don't expect yourself to stop procrastinating straight away! Start by making small steps and know that every step you take will get you closer to where you want to be.

Top tips for beating procrastination:

1. STOP trying to do too much at once! Break bigger tasks down into smaller, more achievable chunks!
2. DO make sure you identify your favourite procrastination activities and excuses and problem solve around these.
3. Finally, definitely DUMP the self-criticism when you procrastinate! It's not going to help you get anything else done and will only make you feel worse!

CHAPTER 20

Self-Compassion – the art of not being a complete bitch to yourself

How many times in your life have you made a silly mistake that anybody could make, or forgotten something that really isn't going to change the entire course of your life, and said to yourself "what's wrong with me, I can't believe I did that!" or "I'm so stupid!". I know I have, too many times! We might all do this, so what's the problem with it? Well, to start with, it's not very compassionate, is it! Would you speak the same way to a friend if they forgot to get the washing in before they left the house and it then started to rain? Probably not, and if you did, it would probably be in jest; but when we speak to ourselves like this, we usually mean it, and we are probably harder on ourselves, more than we actually realise.

So what is self-compassion? Self-compassion is basically the practice of being kind and understanding towards yourself when you're faced with difficult circumstances or when we've made a mistake – as the title of the chapter says, pretty much the art of not being a complete bitch to yourself. Easier said than done, right?! Imagine you're having a really crap day and you're sitting on the sofa in your comfy oversized hoody, watching Netflix and eating a box of Cadbury's Milk Tray. After half an hour, you're criticising yourself, calling yourself lazy and reminding yourself of everything you needed to get done today but haven't. That, my friend, is NOT self-compassion. Self-compassion is kind of like imagining your best friend coming down to sit next to you and handing you the next box of chocolates!

Self-compassion is all about being kind to yourself during those less-than-ideal moments in your life. If you find it difficult to be compassionate with yourself, your childhood trauma might have something to do with this. People with a history of trauma tend to display lower levels of self-compassion. They are more likely to engage in negative self-talk and self-criticism, which can exacerbate feelings of anxiety, depression, and low self-esteem (Gilbert, 2010). However, by being more compassionate towards ourselves, we can begin to heal these old wounds and create a sense of safety, acceptance, self-love, and ultimately be a bit kinder to ourselves.

Self-compassion as articulated by Dr Kristin Neff (2003) consists of three main components:

1. Self-kindness: Treating yourself with care and concern, rather than harsh judgement or self-criticism. Showing ourselves kindness encourages us to be more gentle and understanding with our own flaws and shortcomings.
2. Common humanity: Understanding that suffering is part of the shared human experience, helping us to feel connected rather than isolated in our pain. Basically, knowing that we aren't the only person in the world who messes things up and feels like crap sometimes!
3. Mindfulness: Mindfulness involves maintaining a balanced awareness of our emotions, allowing us to observe our thoughts and feelings without judgement or suppression.

Together, these components create a supportive environment for healing, particularly for those with childhood trauma.

Compassion-Focused Therapy (CFT) was developed by Dr Paul Gilbert as an approach to help individuals struggling with high levels of shame and self-criticism. It integrates cognitive-behavioural techniques with mindfulness practices and emphasizes the importance of developing compassion toward oneself and others. Gilbert identifies three primary systems critical for emotional regulation:

- The Threat System: This system is activated in response to a perceived danger, leading to feelings of anxiety, anger, or fear. People with a history of childhood trauma may have an overactive threat system, making it challenging for them to feel safe and secure.
- The Drive System: This system motivates us to seek rewards, goals, and pleasure. However, for those who have experienced trauma, this drive often becomes skewed, leading to compulsive behaviours as a means of coping with feelings of inadequacy or seeking validation.
- The Soothing System: This system promotes feelings of safety, calm, and warmth. CFT aims to enhance the functioning of the soothing system through self-compassion practices, essential for individuals with a traumatic background.

Using Gilbert's framework, we can integrate self-compassion practices into our own healing journeys. Firstly, we can recognise negative self-beliefs inherited from childhood trauma and challenge them with self-compassionate statements. If we grew up in an environment where we were frequently criticised, we can use statements such as "I am good enough just the way I am" or "I am loveable" to challenge the negative beliefs from our childhood. We challenge these beliefs by looking at what evidence we have for them, and what evidence we have that goes against them.

We can also engage in compassionate imagery, whereby we create a "compassionate self" or "compassionate figure" that embodies love, safety, and support. If you grew up in an environment where you didn't have a nurturing, supporting or understanding figure, engaging in compassionate imagery can be a powerful way to fill that void. By visualising a compassionate self or caring figure, you can invite the qualities of love, safety and kindness into your inner world.

This compassionate figure could be a family member or friend who shows kindness and compassion. It could also be a fictional character from a film, TV show or book. It doesn't matter who your compassionate figure is, as long as they're, well…compassionate! If you're being hard on yourself, ask yourself what your compassionate figure would say to you. Would they be as hard on you as you're being, or would they give you the understanding and care that you need? When you find that you're being tough on yourself, try and engage in guided imagery to connect with this compassionate figure and allow it to nurture your inner child. This practice helps to repair the absence of compassion you may have experienced in childhood, offering a new source of comfort and reassurance.

Another way to use self-compassion to heal your inner child is to practise mindfulness and self-soothing techniques. Mindfulness in self-compassion terms means observing your thoughts and emotions without getting swept away by them. It's kind of like the difference between trying to surf a huge wave if you're just a beginner and sitting on the beach and watching the wave crash. The wave is still there, but we can choose whether we're actually drowning in it or observing it. Mindfulness helps us to become more aware of our emotional states, and self-soothing techniques, such as deep breathing, positive affirmations, or journalling, can help to comfort our inner child.

Finally, have you ever thought about writing a love letter to yourself? I can already hear you saying "what the hell, why would I ever do that?"! Well, if you imagine you're writing it to your best friend, but your best friend is actually you, you can write all of the things that you like about yourself, and all of your positive points, and just generally what an amazing human being you are (because you are!). Try and write this when you're in a good, positive mood, put it away somewhere and read it when you're having a bad day.

The art of self-compassion is like saying let's just be friends with ourselves. Life is messy and hard enough as it is, it would probably be boring if it wasn't! But instead of criticising yourself whenever you've had a bad day, try being your own best friend instead! Remember, caring for your inner child is the foundation of true self-compassion. Just as a young child needs love, patience and understanding to heal from wounds and grow stronger, so do our adult selves. When we nurture our inner child with kindness and acceptance, we create a safe space for healing and growth. Embracing self-compassion means honouring that younger part of ourselves, listening to its needs and reconnecting with the innocence and vulnerability that may have been lost through childhood trauma. When we truly embrace our inner child with compassion, we open the door to a more authentic and resilient life.

Top tips to be more compassionate with yourself:

1. STOP being hard on yourself when you're having a rough time – it won't make you feel any better!

2. DO use compassionate imagery and have a compassionate figure in your mind for when you're struggling to be kind to yourself. Ask yourself what they would say.

3. DUMP the negative beliefs or the icky feeling about being kind to yourself. If you can't be kind to yourself and treat yourself with compassion, love and respect, then how can you expect anyone else to?

CHAPTER 21

Communication in Relationships

This probably won't be a big surprise to you, but our inner child can have a big (HUGE in fact!) impact on our relationships as adults. And this doesn't just extend to romantic relationships, it can also impact our friendships, colleagues, and even how we interact with strangers (ever seen two people who have never met having a huge argument in the middle of a supermarket – that's two wounded inner children!). The wounded inner child can leave a lasting imprint on how we connect with others, and our attachment styles shape our relational patterns and emotional responses (go back to the chapter on attachment styles if you skipped it!).

When the inner child is wounded (and as we've already covered, most of our inner children are wounded in some way!), we can get into unhealthy patterns in relationships. Have you ever noticed that you go for the same types of people or respond in the same unhelpful ways in particular situations? When we do this, it is usually our inner child replaying old patterns from our childhood. If we were lacking something when we were a child, whether it was love, physical affection, approval, or if we learnt that love was conditional in some way, we can sometimes find ourselves gravitating towards relationships where we also feel we have to work for that person's love/approval. When we are with someone who makes us feel as though love is conditional, this takes us back to our childhood, as we try to win that person's love/ approval, because if we do, it's as if our younger self has finally won our parents' love and approval. In essence, it's kind of like we keep trying to create a better ending to our childhood story.

Have you ever seen anyone in a relationship with someone who you can see treats them badly and you've wondered why they put up with it? Or perhaps you've been in that situation yourself before and have even asked yourself the same question. Well, if we weren't provided with the love or affection we needed as a child, we will accept less than we deserve as an adult, as we feel so starved of these things that we will accept even the tiniest part of them, because hey, some love and affection is better than none. Basically, if our emotional needs weren't met as a child, it makes complete sense that we try to get them met as an adult. We will keep attracting the same relationships with the same people, the same situations with the same Daves, which will ultimately lead to the same heartbreak. I know you're now thinking "well this sounds shit", but it doesn't have to be. This is actually an opportunity to see where your inner child is wounded and begin healing. Because until we heal the wounds of our inner child, we will continue to relive the same unhealthy cycles, again and again.

As well as attracting the same people, you might have noticed that you react in the same way to similar situations in different relationships. These could include behaviours such as needing constant reassurance and validation, making your partner jealous, giving them the silent treatment and withdrawing love and affection, or even the good old throwing a temper tantrum when things don't go your way. Maybe you've even reflected on your behaviour after completely losing your shit over something that later on seemed not that big a deal. Have you ever caught yourself thinking "why did I say/do that?! What's wrong with me?!". Well, the inner child is always terrified of one thing, and that's abandonment. Our younger selves are terrified of being left alone, and when something happens that makes our inner child feel as though she could be abandoned, she acts out and sometimes creates merry hell. And until we acknowledge our younger self, connect with her and get to the route of her pain, the same story will continue to play out.

One of the main things impacting our relationships (and not just romantic relationships, pretty much every relationship we have!) is communication and how we resolve conflict. Think about it. Communication is kind of like a bridge. It's a link that connects our thoughts, feelings and intentions with those we care about. Every time you communicate, you're sending a message. However, if our tone changes in the delivery of that message, or if we say something that's likely to be misinterpreted, there's going to be a problem. As we all know, communication isn't just about what we say, it's also about how we say it. I'm sure we have all been on the end of someone saying to us "it's not what you said it's the way you said it"! Tone, body language and even our choice of words can carry "hidden messages". You know the time you said "it's fine" to somebody whilst you were rolling your eyes with your arms crossed? Let's be honest, you probably weren't fine! But ask yourself, what is it that stops you from actually being honest and explaining why you're not fine? Usually, there is some sort of fear that we don't want to confront. If you tell somebody how you really feel, are you afraid of their reaction? Are you scared you'll be abandoned? Are you worried they won't see it from your point of view? When it comes to communication, we can only explain something from our perspective in an assertive but polite way, and how other people respond is down to them. At the end of the day, we only have control over how we communicate and our own behaviours; we can't control other people's responses.

When you're trying to get your point across, try to use "I" statements instead of "you" statements. By this I mean, when you're talking about how you feel, start with "I" rather than you. For example, saying "I've noticed that I feel hurt when you do x/y/z", instead of "you always do x/y/z". Taking responsibility for how you feel when somebody in your life does something that bothers you goes a long way and wording it in this way means there is a big difference in your tone of voice.

We also want to be careful that we aren't just stating facts that have no real meaning. For example, "you never empty the dishwasher" or "you always leave your clothes on the bathroom floor". By doing this, it comes across as though it is an attack on the person, rather than explaining how those things make you feel. When somebody feels as though they are being attacked, their natural instinct is to defend themselves, and this is probably going to end up in an almighty row! By explaining your feelings behind these facts, you're much more likely to end up with a resolution that doesn't end up in an argument.

We also need to be aware of our own patterns and how we resolve conflict. If we weren't taught how to manage conflict effectively as a child, this is going to impact our ability to do so as an adult. If we were taught to suppress our feelings as a child, then we might resort to stonewalling and giving the silent treatment during disagreements. On the other hand, if we were encouraged to express our feelings but watched our parents shout and scream at each other on a regular basis, we may find ourselves resorting to aggressive communication styles or becoming excessively confrontational when faced with conflict. This learned behaviour can create unhealthy cycles where our relationships become battlegrounds instead of safe spaces.

The first step towards healing is (as always!) recognising the impact of the wounded inner child and understanding how it is shaping your current thoughts and behaviour patterns. When you notice something in your relationship provoking an extreme emotional response in you, use your favourite method to connect with your inner child and ask her how she's feeling. Did this situation remind you of something in your childhood? If so, what happened? How did it make you feel? What did you take from this situation? For example, if you were constantly criticised over small things as a child, and your partner then makes a similar comment, it may trigger the same deep-seated feelings of inadequacy or fear of rejection. This reaction can lead to disproportionate anger or sadness, which seem unrelated to the current situation. By gently engaging with your inner child, you can begin to understand that these feelings stem from past experiences rather than the present moment. Once you acknowledge and validate those feelings, you might find it easier to communicate your needs and boundaries to your partner constructively. Instead of reacting defensively, you can express your feelings calmly, explaining that the remark triggered old wounds, and you can invite your partner to work with you on creating a more supportive environment. This process not only enables healing within yourself, but also deepens the emotional connection and understanding in your relationship.

If you find yourself becoming jealous, insecure or find it difficult to trust your partners in relationships, you might be carrying the trust wound. Again, connecting with your inner child can help find out why she is feeling insecure and untrusting. If you have concrete reasons and evidence as to why you don't trust your partner, that's a completely different scenario that requires a sit down conversation. However, if you have absolutely no reason to not trust your partner and are only basing your lack of trust on past wounds, then these can also be addressed by connecting with your inner child and offering her reassurance and compassion. By gently revisiting these childhood wounds, you can begin to understand how they've shaped your perceptions and reactions today. You might want to journal and ask yourself some questions to help facilitate reflection and healing around the trust wound in relationships. Some questions you might want to ask yourself are:

- What specific childhood experiences contributed to my current sense of trust or distrust in relationships?
- How did my parents or caregivers or early relationships demonstrate trustworthiness or lack thereof?
- What fears do I have related to trusting others? How do these fears show up in my current relationships?
- In what moments do I feel most secure and trusting in my relationships? What is happening in those moments?
- Are these instances where I have trusted someone and was hurt?
- What beliefs do I hold about myself that influence how I trust or distrust others?
- How do I react when someone has broken my trust? Are there any patterns I can notice?
- What small steps can I take toward building trust in my current relationships?
- What does my inner child's voice say about trust? What reassurance does she need?
- What affirmations or compassionate statements can I repeat to myself to enable healing of my trust wound?

When answering these questions, be as honest as possible. This is a safe space for your healing. Take your time and allow yourself to explore your feelings without judgement. Remember, your inner child's truth is valid and worth hearing. When you begin to confront these old wounds, it might be that you realise that your current feelings are more of a reflection of your past, and not your present.

We all have an inner child that needs tending to, and our childhood experiences can sometimes lead to chaos in our adult relationships. But the next time you find yourself reacting disproportionately in a situation with your partner, take a minute to check in with your younger self. Nurturing our inner child with kindness allows us to rewrite the narratives that keep us stuck in patterns of doubt and insecurity, which enables us to have deeper connections and better relationships in our lives.

Top tips for managing communication in relationships:

1. STOP attacking the person and try and communicate how something is making you feel instead of telling them everything they have ever done wrong!
2. DO connect with your inner child to find out what exactly it is that has triggered her. Provide her with some love and reassurance and then calmly communicate your feelings to your partner.
3. DUMP the unhealthy patterns of behaviour in your relationships and find calm and diplomatic ways to resolve conflict.

CHAPTER 22

People-Pleasing and Setting Boundaries – Yes, no is a word

Now let's move on to stopping the people-pleasing and setting boundaries, something that feels harder than not watching the next episode on your latest Netflix series and finally going to bed after THAT cliffhanger ending!

Boundaries are basically about knowing what's okay and what's not. They help us protect our time, energy and feelings, and are essential for maintaining our mental health (and sanity!). What's interesting when it comes to our ability and willingness to set boundaries is how this struggle often ties back to our inner child and any childhood trauma we might have carried into adulthood. If you grew up in a household where saying "no" just wasn't an option, you probably find it difficult to set boundaries as an adult. If you were taught that your feelings didn't matter or that you had to please everyone, this can lead to a deep-seated fear of rejection in adulthood. Perhaps you had a narcissistic parent who made everything about them. If that's the case, your younger self has pretty much learnt that your needs come second to theirs, which as an adult translates to your needs come second to other people's, full stop.

In your childhood, if you felt like you had to be the "good girl", and always say "yes" to everything, inside you might have been shouting, "but I don't want to!". It might have even been that you needed to say yes to things to keep yourself safe. Perhaps you knew that there would be consequences or a punishment if you said no, so saying yes became a survival mechanism. Not being allowed any autonomy growing up can often lead to a difficult relationship with boundaries as adults. If as a child we had to say yes to everything and do what we were told in order to not disappoint or anger a parent or caregiver, as adults we're often scared of being rejected or disappointing people, so we tend to end up as a people-pleaser and let people walk all over us.

Another thing that might prevent you from setting boundaries is not actually knowing what your needs are. This might sound strange, but if you have grown up in an environment where your needs weren't considered or where your needs were always at the back of the queue, how do you even know what your needs are? You have probably spent your whole life putting other people first without even thinking about putting yourself first. If this is the case, you might need some time to sit down and actually reflect about what it is you need and how you're going to get it.

So, how do we stop the people-pleasing, set some boundaries and stop being Dave's metaphorical doormat? First of all, you need to recognise that it's perfectly okay to have limits. Think of it as putting on your oxygen mask before helping others. You are not responsible for everyone else's happiness. If Dave calls and wants to see you, that's great, but if it's at a time that isn't convenient for you, it doesn't mean you have to move heaven and earth just to make sure that you can see him at the time that's convenient for him just to make him happy. Instead, you could try saying, "I'd like to see you too, but that time doesn't work for me, can we work out another time that suits both of us?" If he has a hissy fit because that isn't good enough for him, then he probably isn't good enough for you!

Thinking about stopping the people-pleasing and saying "no" to somebody can often trigger our nervous systems to go into the fight/flight response. We might feel as though saying yes keeps us safe and prevents us from feeling that rush of anxiety and fear when it comes to setting a boundary, but in fact we are just keeping ourselves stuck in a never ending cycle. If this resonates with you, try and start small. Try starting with a person you feel more comfortable with and use small statements like, "I can't do dinner tonight, but I'd love to reschedule for another time". Be brave and test the waters and gradually move on to setting more difficult boundaries (with more difficult people!).

If you're worried about setting a boundary, ask yourself what it is that is stopping you from doing this. If you're worried about that person rejecting you and not wanting to see you again, ask yourself what evidence you have for that thought. A true friend is not going to never see you again or think badly of you if you can't do something they have asked you to do, and you know what, if they don't ever see you again, it probably says more about them than it does about you! If it's a fear of the person you are trying to set a boundary with hitting the roof when you say no and giving you absolute hell, again, that says more about them than it does about you. You can only remain calm and stand your ground in a polite and diplomatic way, and whatever they choose to say or however they choose to behave is a reflection of them and their character. Have you ever thought that maybe Dave (or whoever that person is in your life who can be HARD WORK!) might be there so you can learn to set some boundaries?!

When it comes to setting boundaries, practise being assertive. This isn't the same as being rude. It's expressing your wants and needs with confidence. Say it with me: "no, thank you!" doesn't require an elaborate explanation, and you don't have to apologise for it! Why do we always feel as though when we tell someone we can't do something, we owe them a lengthy explanation as to why we can't? We seem to think we need to tell them our entire life story just to justify why we can't look after Joey after school on Tuesday. Perhaps you always say yes to people because you feel guilty if you can't do something or can't help someone out with something. Now, I'm not saying don't ever do anything for anyone and never help people when they need it! But what I am saying is if you do this all the time and constantly say yes to everyone, where does this leave you if you never look after yourself? Probably exhausted and burnt out! And when you're exhausted and burnt out, you won't be able to help people when they actually do need it! By being more assertive and setting boundaries, you'll be putting your own needs first meaning that you are able to help other people at the times you can.

Another thing that can be helpful when it comes to people-pleasing and setting boundaries is making time to reflect. It's useful to look back at your inner child and think about why certain situations make you hesitate. If there's a time where you felt as though you can't set a boundary and aren't able to say no to somebody, ask yourself whether this reminds you of another time where you tried to do this and there was a negative outcome. Perhaps you felt unheard when you were a child when you didn't want to do something, and that fear of not being heard is coming back now as an adult if you say no to someone. Remind yourself that that was then, and this is now, and not every situation is the same. You have control over your decisions as an adult, and how somebody else chooses to react to your decisions is not your responsibility. Journalling can help you explore these feelings and look deeper into the connections between your experiences.

Stopping being a people-pleaser and setting boundaries can feel a bit scary (actually no let's be honest, it can be bloody scary depending on who we are setting the boundary with!), but it really is crucial in order for us to sustain healthy relationships and our own emotional wellbeing. While our childhood experiences and inner child may influence our ability to set boundaries, they don't have to dictate our future. So, the next time you find yourself getting stressed over setting limits, remember: you're nurturing that little girl inside you who deserves to be heard!

Top tips for stopping the people-pleasing and setting some boundaries:

1. STOP saying yes to everything and everyone, you will only exhaust yourself which isn't helpful for you or anyone else!
2. DO practise setting boundaries and start with smaller easier boundaries and build your confidence from there.
3. DUMP the unhelpful beliefs around what it means about you if a decision you make disappoints someone – you aren't responsible for everyone else's emotions!

CHAPTER 23

Are you scared of being alone?

Right, I'm just gonna put it out there. Are you seeing Dave because he's fit, funny and treats you how you deserve to be treated? Really? Or are you just scared that if you do show him the door, you'll be completely alone and you'll never meet anyone else again? One thing I hear time and time again from my clients who are accepting less than they deserve is "but I don't want to be on my own". But let me ask you this, even if you were alone, what is so bad about that?

If we think about it from an inner child perspective, as we've already mentioned, the inner child is terrified of being abandoned, so does the thought of telling Dave to do one bring all of those unhealed abandonment wounds to the surface? This brings us to an uncomfortable truth, which is that many of us fear loneliness, not only because of the void it creates in our lives, but also because of the deep-rooted pain it can unearth. Does it make you feel as though you're unloveable, unworthy, not good enough? Whatever it is, these beliefs can mess with our heads, leading us to believe that "being alone" is the same as "being abandoned".

In order to truly get to the bottom of what it is you don't like about being alone, we need to connect with our inner child (no surprise there!). Feeling abandoned can stem from a parent leaving and no longer seeing us, a loved one passing away, or other events that left us feeling abandoned. Was there a time when you were younger when you were alone that has now left you associating being alone with a negative feeling? Perhaps you were isolated if your parents believed you had misbehaved. It could even have been that you were regularly sent to your room or told you couldn't join in with a family game or event due to your behaviour. This may have left you feeling emotionally and physically abandoned with a lack of connection when you really needed it. Now fast forward to your adult life, how has this fear of abandonment and loss of connection manifested? Are you clingy in relationships because you're afraid of being abandoned? Or do you stay in relationships with people like Dave because you think that some connection is better than no connection, even though you know he isn't treating you very well?

But what if you could learn to embrace being alone instead of fearing it? What if solitude became your sanctuary and a place for healing rather than a threat? And this doesn't just apply to bad relationships. It also applies to people who just struggle being on their own in general. For example, you might dread the house being empty because you just don't know what to do with yourself with no one else around. Or you might dread being alone because that's when your negative or anxious thoughts start to surface. It's usually in these moments of silence that the feelings of self-doubt and unworthiness might rear their heads, and confronting these feelings can feel overwhelming. Remember that being on your own doesn't mean you ARE alone! It doesn't mean that you are unworthy of love or connection, or any of the other things that your negative thoughts are telling you. This is an opportunity for you to truly get to know yourself. "But I don't know what to do on my own" is something I frequently hear from my clients. But let me tell you this, my friend, there is a whole world of things out there you can do on your own!

First of all, let's think of some healing hobbies:

Gardening: Planting seeds and nurturing them mirrors our own journey of healing. As we tend to our plants, we're reminded that growth takes time and patience. The act of caring for something outside of yourself can provide us with a sense of fulfilment and connection to the world.

Writing: Use journalling as a way to express your thoughts and emotions. Write letters to your inner child, encouraging her or letting her know it's safe to feel and have emotions. Creative writing, whether it be poetry, short stories, or even letters you never intend to send, can be an outlet for your feelings and a method for understanding your thoughts more deeply. You can also write down goals or aspirations, and revisit them on a regular basis to monitor your progress.

Painting or crafts: Art doesn't require rules, only your feelings. The colours and shapes you project onto the page can become a reflection of your inner world, allowing you to explore your emotions or release pent up energy.

Physical activity: Get your blood pumping and get some endorphins – the happy hormone! Go for a run, watch an exercise video on YouTube or turn the music up and have a dance party. There's nothing better than singing at the top of your voice to your favourite song (whilst nobody is listening of course!).

Learn something new: Find a new class or look online and teach yourself about something you've always been curious about. Whether it's cooking, watching make-up tutorials or learning a new language, gaining new skills is always fulfilling.

Declutter: Look around your house, there's usually at least one cupboard (or room!) that could do with a declutter.

One way I love to help my clients integrate these activities is called five fun goals. These are five fun (well usually fun!) things you can do on your own. They are usually practical things you can actually do when you're feeling stressed or low. They don't have to be huge activities, just small things you can pick up when you need to. Let me give you an example:

1. Complete rubix cube (old school but why not!)
2. Learn something new (be specific about what it is you're going to learn)
3. Create a vision board
4. Bake a cake
5. Suduko, crossword, or any other mind puzzle you enjoy

Sometime's it's useful to include activities that engage your hands and your mind, so that you aren't doomscrolling whilst doing something that is meant to be good for you. Plus, it's always good to get off our phones and engage in something else sometimes. I know all of these might not sound fun to everyone, but make it your own! Once you accomplish one of your five fun goals, you can then switch it to a new one.

If you truly get to know yourself, know what you like doing and are able to confront any uncomfortable feelings through journalling, or any other ways you like to use to connect with your inner child, you'll soon see that being alone is nothing to fear. Too often, people give up their lives for a relationship and forget who they really are. And of course, when this happens, you aren't going to want to lose that relationship because it has become your whole world. You become more likely to put up with crappy behaviour from them, because it's all you have. Whereas if you hold onto the things you like doing, still enjoy your own company, have your own life with your own hobbies, aspirations and goals, you'll be less likely to tolerate Dave's crap, because guess what, if you do tell him where to go, you still have the most important person – YOU! And something else to mention here, is that the story doesn't end after the worst thing happens. What I mean by that is, if you lose the person you love but who also doesn't treat you properly anyway, yes you will be upset and hurt, but your story doesn't end there. Even if you feel as though you are in the deepest, darkest hole you've ever been in, there will be a day where the tears are less, your chest isn't hurting as much, and you will begin to heal, and begin a new story.

So the next time you find yourself wondering if being alone means being lonely, remember, it's the perfect opportunity to truly heal yourself and dance to the terrible music you're too embarrassed to listen to in front of anyone else, and to finally find and become your true authentic self. And screw putting up with anyone who makes you feel any less than you deserve. Remember, not everyone you lose is a loss!

Top tips for managing the fear of being alone:

1. STOP accepting less than you deserve from certain relationships or friendships because you're scared of being alone.
2. DO find some things you enjoy doing and connect with your inner child to find out why you fear being alone.
3. DUMP the idea that being alone means you ARE alone and unworthy; being on your own is a time to get to know yourself and do whatever the hell you want to do!

CHAPTER 24

Positive Affirmations

I'm not going to lie, the very first time I came across positive affirmations, I thought it was a bit woo woo. I mean, how can speaking to yourself positively make you feel better? But how wrong I was!

So what are positive affirmations and why are they so important?

Positive affirmations are personal phrases or statements that we repeat to ourselves that, over time, help us to change our deeply ingrained (and very unhelpful!) thought patterns. They help us to improve our mental attitudes towards ourselves and are an important tool for our own personal growth.

If you think the idea of saying something positive to yourself feels awkward or just a bit icky, ask yourself why that is. Are you not used to saying positive things to yourself? If not, why not? What emotions and thoughts come up for you if you compliment yourself? Does it make you feel uncomfortable? Do you feel like saying something positive to yourself makes you arrogant? Is there any shame attached to saying something positive to yourself? If you notice any uncomfortable feelings arising, it might be helpful to think about where this stemmed from. Is there an inner child wound buried deep inside you that makes it difficult to be positive about yourself?

If you had parents whose primary love language wasn't words of affirmation, and you didn't have consistent praise and compliments when you were growing up, it might feel unusual and uncomfortable speaking to yourself in a kind and positive way. If you experienced trauma in your childhood, it has likely impacted how you feel about yourself, meaning that you might find it difficult to see anything positive about yourself. Whatever the reason is, it's important to acknowledge it and make some space for it. These wounds came from your childhood, and to gloss over it doesn't provide your inner child with any validation. Remember it is absolutely fine to feel uncomfortable when thinking about using positive affirmations, but don't let that discomfort prevent you from trying!

Another reason people sometimes struggle with the idea of positive affirmations is that they don't believe that using them will have any impact on their daily lives. However, studies have shown that we are able to change our thought patterns, emotions and behaviours through the consistent use of positive affirmations (Sherman & Cohen, 2006).

When you begin to use positive affirmations, it's important that they are specific to the wounds you are working on. For example, if you are working on abandonment wounds, affirmations such as "I am loveable" and "I am worthy" may be helpful for you. Ask yourself what childhood wounds you are trying to heal, and what negative beliefs you hold about yourself that you would like to be different. If you constantly feel as though you're not good enough, how do you want to feel? I'm guessing you want to feel good enough! If this is how you want to feel, then this is your affirmation! If you constantly feel as though you are a failure, you might want to use affirmations such as "I am enough just the way I am, I am strong, I am capable".

When we repeat our positive affirmations on a regular basis, over time our brains begin to rewire as we start shifting our attention from the negative to the positive. No matter how old we are, our brains are always able to change – this is known as neuroplasticity.

Our thoughts are malleable, and our mind will believe what we tell it, which is why if we spend years telling ourselves that we are a failure or that we aren't loveable, we actually believe it. And if believing it wasn't enough, we then begin to look for evidence to support our negative beliefs, so over time they become more and more entrenched. For example, if you have a negative view of yourself, and then you apply for a job you don't get, you are likely to use this as evidence to support your negative view of yourself. You might say things like "I knew I wouldn't get it anyway, I'm not intelligent/good enough for that". When we have these thoughts, they have an instant effect on our emotions, and thoughts like that don't exactly make us feel very good! We're likely to feel low, depressed, and just downright miserable. And then what happens when we're miserable? Yes, you've got it, our thoughts are even more negative! So instead of jumping to the negative straight away and feeling worse, how about saying to yourself "that wasn't the right job for me, I am worthy and capable, and I won't let this setback stop me from searching for another job".

It can be helpful to integrate your affirmations into your daily routine. For affirmations to be effective and to create a change, we need to use them regularly and consistently, rather than just as and when we remember. You might find it helpful to recite your affirmations first thing in the morning after you have woken up. This might make you feel like you're getting the day off to a good start. It might be that you find it more useful to repeat them before you go to bed. Find a time that suits you, in a quiet place where you won't be disturbed. Make sure you speak them aloud, and when you speak the words, make sure you mean them (even if you're not convinced yet, fake it until you make it!) and try and feel the emotions these affirmations bring up for you. For example, if your affirmation is "I am good enough and worthy of new and exciting opportunities", you might feel a sense of pride for being good enough, or a sense of excitement for the good things coming your way. It's imperative to say the affirmations with meaning and conviction and feel the emotions, as if we don't allow ourselves to feel these emotions in our body, we are likely to still be stuck in repeated cycles of negativity and unhelpful patterns of thought.

When creating your affirmations, it is important that you create them in the present tense and use "I am" statements. If we talk about ourselves in the present tense, we are telling ourselves that we are already confident and capable (or whatever your affirmations are!), rather than telling ourselves that we will be these things in the future. By doing this, we are giving ourselves a confidence boost and reminding our brains that these statements are already true.

Something else that you might find useful to do alongside your affirmations is a vision board; a visual representation of your hopes and dreams of everything you want to achieve. Remember when you were a child and used to cut out pictures from magazines and use a Pritt stick to glue them all together? It's a bit like that, but the adult version! Find images of the things you want in your life, or things that represent what you want in your life and start arranging them together on a poster like board. As well as images, you can include motivational quotes that will inspire you to aim towards your goals. Make sure you place your completed vision board in a place where you will see it on a daily basis, as having a regular reminder of your goals and aspirations will only help you build a positive attitude.

Positive affirmations are powerful tools that can facilitate the healing of our inner child. By consciously replacing negative beliefs with uplifting, positive statements, we can rewrite our narratives and gain a sense of hope and self-acceptance. And don't worry about feeling stupid whilst you're talking to yourself, we all need to sit down and have a good talking to ourselves from time to time!

Top tips for using positive affirmations:

1. STOP telling yourself that you are a failure or that you're not good enough, this is NOT going help you build a healthy mindset!
2. DO use your positive affirmations regularly and consistently! Consistency is the key to change!
3. DUMP the scepticism towards positive affirmations, everything is worth a try!

CHAPTER 25

When our emotions are high, our clarity and rational thinking is low

How many times in your life have you absolutely lost your shit over something completely irrational and later on felt a bit...well, a bit of an idiot for maybe just possibly overreacting? Maybe you felt really angry with a particular person or at a certain situation, and had constant thoughts consuming you about that person or situation? When this has happened, how many times have you noticed that when you felt less angry and more calm later on, the volume of thoughts you had dramatically decreased, and you were left with the thought of "what the hell was I thinking?". This is because when we are in an elevated state of emotional arousal, we have access to more thoughts, and basically as the title says, when our emotions are high, our clarity and rational thinking is low.

Many of us have experienced moments when our emotions took over, clouding our ability to think clearly. It might be that you've had a bad day at work and you get home and your partner hasn't done the washing up that they promised they would do. All of a sudden you can't stand the sight of them and remember everything they've ever done in the past that's pissed you off! Sound familiar?

To understand why we struggle with rational thinking when our emotions are running high, we need to touch on a little neuroscience. Our brain processes emotions and rational thought in different areas. When we experience intense feelings – such as anger, sadness, or fear – the amygdala, which is part of our limbic system, kicks into gear. This is the part of the brain that's responsible for our fight or flight response. In these moments, the amygdala often engages the emergency brakes on rational thought, which primarily relies on the prefrontal cortex. Essentially, when emotions take the wheel, rational thinking is pushed to the backseat.

So what does this mean for us? When we feel overwhelmed by our emotions, we tend to react impulsively rather than rationally. These reactions can lead us to decisions we regret, hurtful words, or behaviours we wouldn't otherwise consider if we were thinking clearly.

For those of us who experienced trauma or neglect during our early years, our emotional responses can become even more pronounced. Childhood trauma often impacts the way we handle feelings and stress as adults. When we endure trauma, our inner child becomes stuck in that distressing moment. This part of us may have developed coping mechanisms that weren't necessarily healthy but were vital for survival in that environment, such as shutting down feelings, acting out, or overreacting to perceived threats.

For example, if you grew up in an environment where expressing anger led to punishment, you might either suppress your anger, or express it explosively when it eventually bubbles to the surface. This suppression can lead to outbursts that seem irrational to those around us. Our inner child, triggered by current situations that remind us of past traumas, sends us into emotional overload with the thought: "I must protect myself!" In those moments, our ability to assess situations rationally takes a hit. If our inner child feels threatened, whether it's from a raised voice, a certain tone, or even a comment that we interpret in the wrong way, our emotional reaction can cause us to perceive these situations as much worse than they may actually be. This heightened state of alertness disrupts our ability to think logically. In turn, our responses become defensive, reactive, and sometimes entirely out of character.

When we're calm and collected, our brain processes information differently. We can weigh the pros and cons, consider the impact of our words, and think ahead to possible outcomes. However, when we're too emotional, our perception can change dramatically, meaning that a small disagreement can go from a simple miscommunication into a full-blown crisis, simply because we're flooded with feelings from our past that resonate with the present conflict.

So how do we manage our emotions in these situations and stay rational?

Well, being able to recognise that our emotions can hinder rational thinking is the first step toward managing our responses more effectively. When you see that stack of washing up that hasn't been done and feel your emotions escalating, take a moment to pause. Close your eyes and take a few deep breaths – inhale for a count of four, hold for four, and exhale for four. This simple strategy can help soothe your nervous system and provide a brief window for the prefrontal cortex to engage, allowing for clearer thinking.

Engaging in mindfulness exercises can also help you develop a greater awareness of your emotions and bodily responses. Try to notice sensations in your body, such as tension in your shoulders or a racing heart. Acknowledge these feelings without judgement, and just accept them without trying to supress them. This awareness can help you create space between emotional reactions and rational thought, giving you the opportunity to choose a more thoughtful response.

In addition, writing can be a powerful tool for processing emotions. Keeping a journal where you can freely express your thoughts and feelings can help you unravel what's going on inside your head. Write about situations that trigger strong emotions and reflect on why they might relate to your inner child and past experiences. Ask yourself what the emotion of the current situation reminds you of. If you feel let down in the current situation but your rational self knows it is something minor, for example a friend cancelling plans for a genuine reason, perhaps this reminds you of a time you felt let down or abandoned in your childhood which is why it is triggering a strong emotional response now. Journalling allows your rational mind a chance to analyse what's going on beneath the surface, connect with your inner child and give her the reassurance and support that she was longing for back then.

Emotions are an essential part of being human; they add meaning to our experiences and help us connect with others. Think about it, our whole lives are pretty much dictated by our emotions, whether it's the excitement of going on holiday, the butterflies of a first date, or the fear when we see a huge spider run across the kitchen floor. However, recognising when our emotions are high and thinking about how it might affect our rational thinking is crucial for improving both our relationships with others and our overall emotional wellbeing.

By understanding the connections between our emotional responses, our inner child, and our past trauma, we can learn to build healthier, more rational responses when faced with challenges in our adult lives. Remember, it's ok to feel those emotions, it's ok to feel annoyed when you see that your partner has left the dirty dishes stacked up like a game of jenga on the kitchen worktop, but with practice, we can learn to respond thoughtfully instead of reacting impulsively and completely losing it!

Top tips for managing your reactions when your emotions are running high:

1. STOP letting your emotions dictate your actions – instead acknowledge your emotions without judgement.
2. DO reflect on your childhood and ask yourself if these emotions come from an earlier time.
3. DUMP the impulsive reactions and engage in some mindfulness exercises or breathing techniques to give your prefrontal cortex time to engage!

CHAPTER 26

Do you feel like you're running out of time?

How many times has it crossed your mind that you're running out of time? That little voice inside your head tells you that you're too old or that it's too late to do that thing you've always wanted to do but never got around to doing. Whether it's finding a meaningful relationship, making new friends or trying something exciting like skydiving, you feel as though the time has passed and it just won't happen or that it's too late to even try.

This fear can stem from our inner child. As children, we constantly absorbed messages about success and happiness that often tied these concepts to age. If we think about our childhood, there was probably a lot of focus on milestones and pressures to achieve things by a certain age. When we started walking, talking, reading and writing are all milestones that people around us would have spoken about. And then think about school, there were SATs, GCSEs, A-Levels. Then there were other social "milestones" like when you got your first boyfriend or girlfriend. Do you remember a time in your younger years where you didn't reach an expected milestone at a certain point? Perhaps you didn't pass a GCSE and had to retake the following year, or did your peers all have boyfriends or girlfriends before you? If there was a negative reaction to any of these situations, it might have left you believing that you were a failure if you hadn't "achieved" something at a certain point. Or maybe you grew up believing that if you hadn't reached a certain milestone by a particular age, that you somehow missed your chance. But why are we attaching a number to whether or not we can be successful or whether or not we can start over again. After all, it's just a number!

It's never too late to start again, and it's never too late to begin building the life you have always wanted, or to start working on that goal you've always wanted to achieve. Let's take a look at people who have achieved things later on in life!

- At 28 years old, JK Rowling was a single parent living on welfare. She was 32 years old (and no, I'm not saying that 32 is later on in life!) when she published her first book, and let's face it, that turned out pretty well for her!
- Vera Wang didn't design her first dress until she was 40 years old.
- Samuel L. Jackson didn't get his first movie role until 46 years old.
- Ray Kroc bought the first McDonald's when he was 52 years old.
- Colonel Sanders opened the first KFC at 62 years old.

And my favourite by far!

- Charlotte Chopin began practising yoga at the age of 50, and in May 2024 was awarded the Padma Shri for defying "age-limiting norms" at the age of 101! Age really is just a number!

And just to add to these…

- It took James Dyson 5126 times to create the Dyson vacuum cleaner, that's 5125 attempts that failed! Now that's what you call perseverance!
- Walt Disney was fired by a newspaper editor because he "lacked imagination and had no good ideas"...I mean, come on!

Imagine what would have happened if all of these people had given up on their dreams, or if they hadn't even attempted them because they felt as though the time had already passed or they had already failed enough times and couldn't take another failure? Imagine a world without Dyson vacuums, KFC, McDonald's, Harry Potter and the magic of Disney! Who can say that their lives would have ever been the same without reading a Harry Potter book or watching a Disney movie growing up? Yet we wouldn't have any of these things if these people had given up or let their age stop them from doing something.

There is nothing worse than the sadness of feeling as though you are wasting your life. We only have one life after all, and why would we not want to make the most of every day we have? This might sound a bit like "you only live once", and whilst this is true, what I actually want us to think about here is why we constantly focus on the time that has passed and what we haven't done with that time, rather than looking at what we have achieved and the positives we have already had in our life, and how we can make the most of the time we have going forward. We might not be able to get yesterday back, but never forget that TODAY is the very first day of the rest of your life. Not yesterday, not tomorrow, today.

Ask yourself what it is that is stopping you from working towards what you want. If you feel as though you're running out of time or that it is too late now, you certainly aren't going to gain any more time by thinking about the time that has already passed! Or maybe the fear of being behind in life is rooted in an experience from your younger self where maybe you were ridiculed or criticised for being "behind". In which case, it might be helpful to connect with your inner child and have a meaningful conversation with her and revisit that difficult time in your life so that you can tell her what she needed to hear at that time and begin healing some old wounds.

Maybe your worry isn't that you haven't achieved a goal you wanted to achieve, but that you have absolutely no idea what you want to do with your life and you don't know where to begin! And this is ok too! Who says you should have your life figured out by 25? 30? 35? 40? Even 50! Why do we feel like when we are a certain age, our life should be sorted? Who is putting a number on this stuff?! Of course, there is Lucy from Pilates who has it all, perfect relationship, 2.4 children, lovely house, good career, and of course not forgetting she always finds time to bake cakes for the school cake sale instead of buying them from the Tesco Express five minutes before the school run. We all know a Lucy from Pilates who puts our lives to shame, but first of all, just because Lucy seems to have it all figured out, it doesn't mean that your life should be like hers. And secondly, most importantly, we always have a view of somebody's life from the outside, but really, we never truly know what somebody's life is really like for them, and what battles they might be facing that we don't know about. So, don't focus on the lives of others around you, stop comparing, and know that you don't have to have it all figured out. As a therapist who has had the privilege of listening to the insights of countless lives, trust me when I say that we're all just winging it!

As well as worrying that the time to achieve our goals has already passed us by, another problem we may encounter is that sometimes we are too attached and too focussed on our goals, that we are unable to stop and live in the present. It is all well and good having a dream to work towards, but if we are so fixated on that that we are unable to see anything going on around us, then we are missing what's going on in the here and now. You might think something like "I'll be happy when I get that job", and constantly think about your future life in that job. There has to be a balance between working towards something that you want in the future, and being present and enjoying the moment you are in. Don't ever give up on your dreams, but remember that life is about the journey – make sure you enjoy it!

So next time you're worried that you're running out of time, remind yourself that you won't get any time back by thinking about the time that has already passed. Instead, focus on the present moment and enjoy the choices you can make today. Embrace your journey of healing and growth, understanding that there's no perfect timeline, only your own unique path.

Top tips for if you're feeling as though you're running out of time in life:

1. STOP thinking that it's too late to do that thing you've always wanted to do! People do miraculous things at all ages!
2. DO think about what it is you want to achieve and ask yourself what is holding you back from this.
3. And finally DUMP the idea that you need to have everything figured out by now!

CHAPTER 27

Tolerating Uncertainty

The comfort zone, let's face it, we're all familiar with it! It's that cosy little hideaway where everything feels safe and predictable. It's where we binge watch our favourite series for the fifth time, scroll mindlessly through social media, stick to our usual routines, or stop at the same petrol station on the way to work because it's familiar to us. It's where we stay in unhealthy relationships and jobs we don't really like because we don't know what life would be like without them. Now don't get me wrong: there's nothing inherently bad about liking routine and safety. But there's a downside as well. Staying in that comfort zone and trying to have certainty over everything for too long can actually hinder our growth, relationships and overall potential. And let's face it, it can get a bit boring!

Before we look more into this, let's take a moment to think about our inner child and how this keeps us avoiding uncertainty and likes us to stay in comfortable situations. As our inner child carries every wound from our childhood, it makes sense that she often craves safety and familiarity and shies away from new experiences that might feel threatening or overwhelming. As adults, we sometimes react to discomfort in ways that can be traced back to childhood experiences. That irrational fear of public speaking? It could stem from a past experience of not being heard or validated. The need to sit in a corner instead of dancing at a party? Maybe it's linked to childhood memories where you felt judged or unworthy. If you were physically or emotionally abandoned by a parent as a child, you might notice you get overly attached to people and try to keep them close to prevent the uncertainty of them leaving.

Understanding these links can help us approach discomfort with a more compassionate mindset so that we are able to be more understanding with ourselves about why we actually need certainty in the first place.

The problem with needing certainty all of the time is the more you have it, the harder it becomes to tolerate situations where you can't be certain. Let's take the petrol station example. You might stop at that particular petrol station on the way to work because you know where it is, it's easy to get in and out of, there's hardly ever a queue so you'll be fine if you're running a few minutes late. But what happens if that petrol station were to suddenly close down? Shock! Horror! We would have to go somewhere else! Maybe somewhere we haven't ever been before! What if it's really busy and makes you late? What if the long reach hoses are really difficult to pull round and you look stupid? And this is just an example about a petrol station! Tolerating uncertainty when it comes to relationships, careers, and anything else with meaning is much harder.

Sometimes we might feel as though the unpredictability of a situation is intolerable to us. We might try to avoid any situation which makes us feel uncertain, as we find the not knowing unbearable. We might believe that we just won't be able to cope with not knowing an outcome to a situation, which can lead us to a pattern of avoidance. For example, if you are worried about a job interview coming up, instead of tolerating the uncertainty of waiting for the interview, and then waiting to find out whether you got the job or not, you may just cancel the interview all together so you don't have to deal with these emotions at all.

People who find it difficult to tolerate uncertainty often engage in self-sabotaging behaviours, as they may deliberately sabotage the outcome of a situation just so that that outcome is now certain to them, even if it is negative. People who find it difficult to tolerate uncertainty often prefer something bad happening right now, rather than waiting and seeing what the eventual outcome of a situation might be. If something bad happens now, at least it is in our control and we are able to do something to deal with it, rather than sit with and tolerate the uncertainty and anxiety that comes with not knowing.

If you are someone who finds it difficult to tolerate uncertainty, you might find that you believe that worrying is actually a positive thing. For example, you might believe that worrying helps you to prepare for anything bad happening, as if you have already predicted it, it can't surprise you and you might feel that you are more able to cope with it. Therefore, worrying, in a sense, is a way of reducing the uncertainty of a situation, as if you have already worried about every possible outcome to that particular situation, surely there won't be any surprises? This then gives us the illusion of control, as we are more likely to feel in control if we have already predicted what is going to happen.

However, if we were to apply some rational thinking to this, does the worry make things any better? Does it change the outcome of that situation? You might believe that by worrying about a situation you have more control over it, but is that really true?

Let's think about this scenario for a moment. If I had a button you could press that would show you exactly what would happen in your life from right this second, up until the day you die, would you press it? Would you really want to know absolutely everything, the good, the bad and the ugly? Perhaps you would think yes, it would be helpful if I knew any bad things that are going to happen in my life, as then I have the chance to change them beforehand. But what if you don't have that ability? What if you are able to know everything in advance, but are completely unable to change it? You might think, ok, well if I can't change it, at least I can be prepared for it. But in reality, what good would it do for you to know about something bad happening five years before it actually happened? Surely you would just spend those five years living in misery and dread, not enjoying anything else in your life because you're waiting for that bad thing to happen. Then let's think about the good things. Would it be helpful for you to know something good that is going to happen to you in five years, surely knowing something good won't do us any harm? Maybe we would think this wouldn't be as harmful as knowing something bad will happen to us, but if we know that something good is going to happen and we really look forward to it, would it take away from living our life in the present, because we are so focussed on the future? Would we really be grateful and appreciative of anything we have now, if we know something amazing is coming up for us in five years' time? Would we be as surprised or excited if we met the love of our life in the paint aisle at B&Q if we already knew we were going to meet them there? Would we really try our best at everything, if we already knew the outcome? Most probably not!

Sometimes we can find it really difficult to tolerate things that are uncertain, but we do it in our everyday lives more than we think. We leave for work at a certain time every day, not knowing 100% whether there will be something that holds us up on our journey, meaning we might get to work later and miss that important meeting we've been preparing for. We cook dinner, not knowing if the phone will ring and distract us, meaning that we burn dinner and have to start all over again. We leave the house to go on a walk, but can never be 100% sure that we won't be hit by a bus! (Ok that one's a bit extreme, but you get what I'm saying!) The point is that we tolerate these situations anyway, without even realising, and the fact is, we can never be absolutely certain about everything in life, and when we try and be certain about everything, it is inevitably going to make us anxious.

When we are trying to increase our certainty, our attention is completely focussed on the future, as we analyse all possible outcomes to a situation, just so that we are able to work out what we can do in response to each outcome, but is this really helpful? And how much time does this take us?! Usually much more time than it's worth!

So how do we reduce our need to be certain about everything all the time? One way to overcome the intolerance of uncertainty is to try to be more aware of the times when you need certainty, and then ask yourself what you are doing to try to achieve it. Are you worrying more and running through every possible scenario in your mind, or are you avoiding something altogether as you can't tolerate not knowing the outcome? If you notice yourself doing these things, ask yourself whether it is helpful that you are worrying, and make the conscious choice to not respond to those worries and that need to be certain. Instead, focus your attention on the present rather than the future. When we are completely focussed on the present, we are not as worried or bothered about the future as our attention is on the here and now, which essentially, is the only thing we have some control over.

If you find that you constantly need certainty over a particular aspect of your life, it might be helpful for you to look more deeply into where this need for certainty came from. Was there a time in your childhood where something was uncertain for you? If you experienced a parent leaving you may have been uncertain about when you were going to see them again. Or if you had a parent whose mood would quickly change, you might have been uncertain about what their mood was going to be like that day and felt as though you were constantly walking on eggshells. Basically, if you grew up with tension, chaos and uncertainty it makes complete sense why you would need certainty now. When you find yourself feeling anxious because you feel uncertain about something, ask yourself how old this feeling is. Does it come from five year old you, or nine year old you? What was going on for you at that time? When you can pinpoint the age of the emotion and the situation surrounding these feelings, it's time to sit down and have a talk with your inner child. Tell her that you completely understand why she feels uncertain and tell her that you are here now. Tell her that you love her and that you will always be here for her, no matter what. Remember, it isn't about helping your inner child to feel certain about everything, it's about telling her that it's ok to feel uncertain at times, it's part of life, but that you will be able to manage whatever happens. If you need to cry and release what you have been holding onto inside, then cry. Just take time to sit and be with your inner child and begin to heal those old wounds you've been carrying.

As we've already mentioned, our core beliefs are built from our experiences and perceptions in our younger years. Our negative core beliefs often come from our comfort zones. "I'm not good enough", "I can't handle that", or "what if I fail?" can all make us feel pretty crap and stop us from even looking at something outside of our comfort zone. Stepping into discomfort often shines a light on these beliefs, which allows us to challenge them. For example, if you are given a new work assignment, you might want to avoid it somehow if there is a voice inside telling you that you'll fail. But if you sit with the uncertainty and the uncomfortable emotions and do the assignment and your boss tells you it's great, you have then proved your negative beliefs wrong. With each uncomfortable experience we face, we build evidence against those beliefs, proving to ourselves that we can indeed handle more than we ever thought possible. Remember, you don't have to leap from the comfort zone right into the deep end. Start small! Maybe it's trying a new café in town, striking up a conversation with someone new, or taking that fitness class you've been curious about. Each small step you take builds your tolerance for uncertainty, making the next step feel slightly easier.

As well as connecting with our inner child and reflecting on our core beliefs, breathing exercises can also help regulate our nervous systems and bring us out of our fight/flight response. When you notice feelings of discomfort begin, take a moment to breathe. Mindful breathing can ground you and help pull you back from the chaotic swirl of emotions. Inhale deeply through your nose for a count of four, hold for four, and exhale through your mouth for a count of four. Repeat this a few times and notice how your body starts to relax. You'll find that your discomfort feels a little more manageable after a few deep breaths.

When you feel uncomfortable and uncertain, it's natural to be hard on yourself, but instead of criticising yourself for feeling anxious or scared, practise self-compassion. Speak to yourself as you would to a friend. Remind yourself, "it's okay to feel this way; this is part of growth." A simple mantra like "I am doing my best" can remind you that discomfort is a sign of progress, not failure.

After going through an uncertain situation, take some time to reflect on the experience. What did you learn? How did it feel? Writing in a journal can help clear out your thoughts and even reveal patterns around what makes you uncomfortable. It can also serve as a record of your growth journey, reminding you of how far you've come when you look back.

Furthermore, we need to make the conscious decision to let this worry go and accept that uncertainty is a normal part of being human. A famous quote by Benjamin Franklin is "in this world, nothing can be said to be certain, except death and taxes", and let's face it, he was right! (But even then, if there is an afterlife, I'm sure there is some room for negotiation!) If we make the decision to let the worry go, we feel more in control of our own responses, and less overwhelmed and anxious about the need to be certain about everything.

And finally, you're not alone on this journey! It's perfectly okay to lean on friends, family, or even a therapist when you're navigating uncomfortable feelings. Share your experiences with trusted people in your life. They may offer insights and encouragement that make facing uncertainty a little easier and remind you that we all feel uncomfortable and uncertain at some points in our life.

At the end of the day, becoming more comfortable with discomfort and uncertainty is a journey, not a destination. It takes time, patience, and a lot of self-love to learn how to embrace the unknown. As you navigate your healing journey, remember to give yourself grace when things feel tough. Your inner child may kick and scream for security and certainty, but remind her that no matter what happens, you will always be there for her, and you will cope with anything that comes your way. Let her know it's okay to take a step into the unknown. You've got this!

Top tips for managing uncertainty:

1. STOP focussing on the future and bring yourself back to the present.

2. DO notice the times when you feel you need to be certain and ask yourself how old this feeling is. Try and pinpoint the memory that this need for certainty comes from and reassure your inner child that you are here for her.

3. And finally, DUMP the need to know the outcome to everything all the time. Life is an unpredictable journey with all sorts of twists and turns, some good, some not so good, but would we really have it any other way?

CHAPTER 28

Toxic relationships and the narcissist – if the man doesn't change, just change the man

So, picture this. You've been seeing Dave for a few months and so far, so good. No, who are you kidding? It's not just good, it's great! He's hot, funny, you can talk to him about anything, he makes you feel like no one else ever has. He treats you so well and you genuinely think he might be the one. Why would you not? You've never had this connection with anyone before! He always replies to you, would never leave you on delivered, and goes out of his way to make time for you.

This. Is. Amazing.

Until one day, he asks about your day, and you innocently tell him about the joke you had with the postman earlier that morning. And then you realise, that was a big mistake.

Because Dave loses his shit.

Big time.

"Why would you be talking to another man? Why would you make another man laugh? Do you fancy him? Is he attractive? Is he more attractive than me? Do you talk to any men you see on the street?"

Woah. Woah. Woah.

What is this? What just happened?

And this is the major red flag where you realise Dave might not be all you thought he was, because from this moment on, you're treading on eggshells wondering when he will lose it again.

But here's the thing, instead of telling him that his reaction wasn't acceptable, you try to be better. You don't tell him to do one. You don't call him out for his jealousy, you don't say "this is not okay". You just try harder. You make a point of not speaking to anyone of the opposite sex, even when in reality you know that they make up half of the population, so they're kind of hard to avoid. You make sure you reply on time because now he's starting to ask why you didn't reply to his message for two hours even though you already told him you had that important meeting at work. You start saying no to seeing your friends because he starts accusing you of seeing them more than him.

You smooth things over, you apologise for being "careless" with your texts, you promise you'll be better. You stop wearing the dress that got a "you're not wearing that out" look. You delete a couple of male numbers from your phone "so it looks less weird". You start checking in more, send a running commentary of your day so he knows where you are and who you're with. You become the ghostwriter of your own life and start scripting every move so he doesn't get scared, and so you don't have to have him bombarding you with questions and losing it again.

For a while, this feels like it's working. But here's the problem: with every tiny surrender, the bar moves. That's how it works. What used to be unacceptable becomes the new normal. The line you thought you'd never cross quietly erodes, step by step, until you can't remember where it was in the first place. You accept a little more, then a little more again, and each time you do it because it feels easier than the fight. It feels safer than the inevitable blow-up.

It feels like this is what you do for love, you put the effort in to keep the person you want in your life.

But what are you really doing? You're not negotiating the relationship, you're negotiating your worth.

When Dave shouts, you don't tell him his behaviour is toxic; you tell yourself you must be careless, irresponsible, too flirty, too ungrateful. You tell yourself how lucky to have someone like him and ask yourself why you're messing it up. You scrub, smooth and edit yourself into the picture he wants, hoping that if you match his script long enough, actual safety and real love will follow.

This is where the inner child sets the scene.

If as a child you grew up in an environment whereby you learnt that love and controlling behaviour are intertwined, you might grow up to see this as normal and be more willing to accept it yourself. Or, if as a child your early experiences with your parents showed you that you're only worthy if you're perfect, or you're unlovable unless you behave, then you might have grown up with core beliefs such as "I am not enough, I'm unlovable", which have created rules for living such as, "I must earn love", or "If I don't try harder, I will be rejected". But these beliefs don't live in your head in neat sentences, they live in your reactions, the immediate impulse to fix, to people-please, and to prove you're worthy.

So when Dave's jealousy lands like a small earthquake, that inner child rises up and says, "See? I was right. I'm not lovable unless I try harder." The adult you then doubles-down on behaviour that will prove the child wrong. You over-apologise, over-explain, over-accommodate, hoping the proof will finally stick and calm the storm. Except it rarely does. Because narcissistic or controlling partners don't respond to proof of worth the way we imagine. They respond to submission and compliance, which simply trains them to ask for more. The harder you try, the more they take, the more you give, the less you get. Trying to prove you're lovable becomes the very behaviour that confirms your original fear: you feel small, invisible and, yes, worthless.

It becomes a vicious cycle:

- A triggering moment happens (a look, a text, a question).
- The inner child feels threatened and whispers the old belief: "You're not enough".
- You respond by trying to prove your worth with concessions and explanations.
- The partner escalates, takes more, or belittles the effort.
- The inner child's belief is reinforced because the outcome feels the same: rejection or instability.
- You feel worse, and the cycle repeats.

Recognising this pattern is the first act of rebellion. Not because you must punish Dave or brand him forever, but because you must stop being the person who proves your worth to someone who's never going to value it properly.

So, how do you change this?

- Firstly, notice the old voice. When you feel the urge to over-explain or to cancel friends, name the feeling: "That's my inner child trying to be safe." Remind yourself that in a loving and trusting relationship, you wouldn't need to cancel your friends because you are being accused of caring about them more.

- Separate proof from love. Real love doesn't require exhaustive evidence. It tolerates boundaries and respects them. You should never have to prove yourself to anyone.

- Start small boundary experiments. You don't have to leave on day one, but you can start saying "no" to things that feel invasive. Watch what happens. If he responds by respecting you, that's information you can use. If he responds by escalating, that's also information. It tells you about his capacity for mature love.

- Reparent your inner child. Was there a situation in your childhood that left you feeling as though you needed to earn love or prove your worth? Connect with your inner child and offer yourself the messages you never got: "You are enough. You deserve respect. You don't have to earn love." Say them aloud. Practise them when you want to go back to people-pleasing.

- Build safety nets. Call a friend before confronting a pattern (I'm sure your friend has already told you that they think Dave's behaviour is toxic!). Have exit plans for conversations that escalate.

And here's the painful truth: sometimes you can't change it. If a man's pattern is to nudge, control and gaslight you until you shrink, telling him to change is often useless unless he's willing to do the hard, internal work himself. You can ask, you can set boundaries, you can insist on respect, but if he refuses or punishes you for asserting yourself, the only sane option is to change the man in your life: leave.

Getting rid of Dave doesn't mean instant healing. You'll still carry your inner child's scars, and the scars from that relationship. But leaving a situation that constantly validates "I am not enough" is an essential step toward rebuilding a different story: one where you teach that inner child that love is not conditional on performance, where your worth is not something you have to argue for. Every time you choose your own boundaries, you feed your inner child a new belief: "I am safe. I am enough, and I will not shrink to keep someone else comfortable."

So when you next meet a Dave, or when your current Dave goes off at a postman joke, listen. And I don't mean listen to the panic that tells you to prove yourself, but to the steadier adult in you who can set limits. Teach your inner child that the bar doesn't have to move; you can stand firm. That's not cold or cruel; it's the beginning of being loved the way you deserve.

Top tips for dealing with toxic behaviour:

1. STOP telling yourself that you need to change or prove your worth to someone for them to love you. You don't have to prove your worth to anyone.
2. DO pay attention to people's patterns and any toxic behaviours you notice. Try to set boundaries and limits when you can and when you feel safe to do so. If you don't feel safe, talk to someone you trust about the situation and get some help.
3. DUMP the narcissist if he doesn't work on himself and change his behaviour. Just dump him.

CHAPTER 29

Oh crap, does this mean my children are doomed for a life of unhealthy core beliefs and a wounded inner child?

S o now we are nearing the end, I bet some of you are probably wondering what all of this means for your children, or perhaps future children if you don't have them yet and would like to one day. Does this mean that every child is doomed for a life of negative core beliefs and a wounded inner child? Well, not quite. Sure, you could be the perfect parent (not that such a thing exists, we all make mistakes), your child could have the perfect life at home, but they may have struggles at school or with their friends. There will always be a struggle somewhere, but the most important thing is helping your child to overcome this and gain the skills and experience they need to take them through life.

Now you have learnt about love languages, it might be helpful for you to be aware of the love languages you use with your children, and ones you may not use as much. You might want to talk to your child and ask them what makes them feel most loved by you. Are your words important to them? If they are, tell them positive things, praise them for their achievements, let them know that you're listening, that you're here if they need you, that they make you smile. Perhaps they value spending quality time with you, in which case you might want to ensure that you set aside a certain amount of time each day for connection, or a weekly activity you can do together. Once you are aware of your own love language and the love language of your child or children, you will be more able to meet their needs and ensure they know how much you love them. Whilst it is important for you to praise your child, it is also just as important to teach them to praise themselves. Let them know that achieving something isn't about your approval, but it's about them seeing the value in their own achievements.

Reflect on your own childhood and relationships with your caregivers. What would you have wanted to be different? What needs did you have that weren't met? Did you feel able to communicate that? As parents, we want to give our children the best lives possible, but that doesn't mean a big house, stacks of toys and expensive holidays. It can mean being there for your children when they need you, knowing that you love them unconditionally and making sure that they know they can come to you for absolutely anything. When we are adults, we generally forget about the possessions that were bought for us, but we remember the time that was spent playing hide and seek, or how we were taken care of when we were unwell, or the time we made cupcakes with our parent or caregiver and were able to lick the bowl (definitely the best part of baking!). It could be that you make up silly songs or games in the car or at bath time, or go for a walk and point out interesting things. The time spent with your children will be more valuable than any possession, so don't beat yourself up if you can't afford the latest thing they want (and there will always be another new latest thing they want!).

What about when your children are really testing your patience (which is pretty much a guarantee at some point in their lives!)? What about when they are purposely pushing our buttons, giving us back chat and just being a general pain in the arse? Something that can be helpful to remember is to always connect before we correct. This means instead of instantly trying to "correct" your child's behaviour, either by shouting, taking away their favourite toy or sending them to their room, actually connect with them and find out what is going on under the surface. What is it they need from you at the moment? All behaviour is a form of communication, and what we really need to understand from our child's behaviour is what they are actually trying to communicate with us. All "attention" seeking behaviours are usually connection seeking behaviours, so if your child is purposely doing something you have asked them a million times not to do and deliberately winding you up, the chances are they already know that they shouldn't be doing that, and they are actually seeking some form of connection from you. If we go back to thinking about love languages, do they need a hug, or are they needing some more quality time with you? Is there something they want to talk to you about but they're unsure how to? Instead of reacting to your child's negative behaviour, try and respond to their needs and find out what it is they need that they are trying to communicate with you. When you find out what this is and are able to meet their needs, the chances are that the connection seeking behaviours will reduce and they will feel more able to communicate with you in the future.

Find regular times to connect and communicate with your child. Some prime times for connection and communication are when they have woken up or when they have finished school. When your child wakes up, you could try asking them how they slept and if they had any interesting dreams. If they have school today, ask them if there is anything they are looking forward to about today, or any friends they are excited to see. When they have finished school, perhaps ask them how their day was, and try asking open questions such as "what did you learn today" or "what was your favourite part of today". By asking open questions, you are giving your child a chance to give you a more detailed and thoughtful response. If we ask closed questions such as "did you have a good day today", we can sometimes just get a short "yes" or "no" response, which doesn't leave much opportunity for connection. Another good time for connection and communication is before your child goes to bed. This gives them a whole day to reflect over and for you to find out more about their life from their perspective. It might be that you ask them about what the best part of their day was, or whether there is anything they are worried about that they would like to talk to you about. If your child finds it difficult to talk, maybe you could have a notebook where they can leave messages in and you can reply to them. This prevents difficult emotions such as embarrassment from getting in the way of them being able to talk to you about important things. If they find it difficult to talk in a sit down face-to-face environment, try going for a walk together, where you can walk alongside your child and listen to them. This way, your child doesn't have to face you if they are talking about something they find uncomfortable, and they might find this way of communicating easier if they are trying to tell you about a problem they are having.

Speaking of problems, when your child tells you about a problem they are having, as parents, our first thought is that we want to rescue them and protect them from everything. And there are times when we might need to do that, but before we do, it can be helpful to ask your child whether they want you to offer them advice, if they need you to get involved or if they need you to just listen. This way, you are letting them think about what they need before jumping in, and if they need your advice, and they manage to solve their problem without you getting involved, this can be a great learning opportunity for them and they will feel more able to come to you and problem solve in the future.

Although we might all aspire to be the perfect parent, it's important that you let your children see you make mistakes – it's part of being human after all! Let them see you apologise, and apologise to them if you do something wrong or react in a way that you wish you hadn't (we all do it!). Let them see you admit that you were wrong, see you work through problems, and ask for help. By modelling positive behaviours, your child will learn that it is ok to make mistakes, and that acknowledging them and apologising is a strength, not a weakness. It's also helpful to be aware of our own double standards when it comes to asking our children to do things. For example, when your child asks you to do something when you are halfway through cooking the dinner or folding the never ending pile of laundry, how many times do we say to them "I'll do it in a minute", or "come back and ask me later", but yet we expect them to put on their shoes and tidy their room as soon as we ask them? When our child sees us doing this, it creates a "do as I say, not as I do" culture, which children very easily pick up on. By being aware of situations like this, we can create a fairer living environment where everyone is able to get their needs met.

When it comes to parenting, only you know what is best for you and your child, but as long as your child knows that they are safe, loved, cared for, and that doing their best is good enough for you, you're already setting the foundations for healthy core beliefs that they will take into adulthood.

Top tips for raising children with good core beliefs:

1. STOP beating yourself up if you aren't able to afford the latest new toy or pair of trainers. Your unconditional love and your time are more important to your child, and will contribute more towards healthy, positive core beliefs than any amount of money will.
2. DO find regular times to connect with your child and ask them open questions about their day and their feelings.
3. DUMP the unrealistic expectations of being the perfect parent 24/7. Nobody is perfect, your best is good enough!

Epilogue

So there we have it, how to stop it, do it, dump them in a nutshell (well, maybe a big nutshell!). Although this is the end of the book, this is actually the beginning for you, the chance to break the cycle and heal those wounds that you know need healing. I'm not going to tell you it will be easy – I know from experience it won't be – but what I can tell you is that it will be worth it to not have to carry this pain you're carrying around with you every day.

Healing your wounds from childhood trauma is a journey, and it might be one that you are on for a while, but just take one step at a time, and only look back to see how far you have come. Of course, there will always be challenges in life, healing your wounds isn't about your inner child never showing up again, it's about knowing your triggers and knowing how to manage her and reassure her when she does.

I'm grateful you have shared this journey with me, and I hope you have found something in this book helpful. No matter where you are in your life at the moment, no matter how dark it feels, no matter how much pain you feel inside, it's always possible to heal. You have made it this far in your life, and you didn't come this far to *only* come this far! So, when the days are dark and you don't know how you're going to get out of this hole you've found yourself in, remind yourself that you have got more strength than you think, you just need to find it. I know I said take one step at a time, but if a step feels too much, crawl, and little by little you will get to the place you need to be.

Life can be hard and painful, but it can also be filled with moments of beauty and amazing opportunities for growth and resilience that remind us of our inner strength and capacity for healing, if we look for them. The truth is that although you aren't always going to be able to control your circumstances in life, you can control how you and your inner child respond to them. Remember that you are not your trauma, and that your childhood does not need to define you.

So go on, heal your wounds, let go of your pain and live the life you always wanted to live. Be the person you've always wanted to be. Go for the job. Start the new hobby. Tell that person NO! Dump Dave if he's not treating you well. And next time you find yourself in an unhealthy situation in your life, remember, you can always

Stop it.
Do it.
Or
Dump them!

References

Ainsworth, M. D. S., Blehar, M. C., Waters, E., & Wall, S. (1978). *Patterns of Attachment: A psychological study of the Strange Situation.* Lawrence Erlbaum Associates.

American Psychological Association. (2015). *APA Dictionary of Psychology (2nd ed.).* Washington, DC: Author.

Bandelow, B., & Friederich, H. C. (2017). *Serotonin and beyond: neurochemistry of anxiety disorders.* European Neuropsychopharmacology, 27(2), 102–122.

Beck, A. T. (1976). *Cognitive Therapy and the Psychopathology of Feeling.* In P. M. Salkovskis (Ed.), Frontiers of Cognitive Therapy (pp. 65–90). Guilford Press.

Blumenthal, J. A., Babyak, M. A., Doraiswamy, P. M., Watkins, L., Hoffman, B. M., Barbour, K. A., ... & Sherwood, A. (2007). *Exercise and Pharmacotherapy in the Treatment of Moderate to Severe Depression.* Psychosomatic Medicine, 69(7), 587-596. DOI: [10.1097/PSY.0b013e3180601469]

Bowlby, J. (1969). *Attachment and Loss: Volume I. Attachment.* Basic Books.

Bradshaw, J. (1988). *Homecoming: Reclaiming and Championing Your Inner Child.* Bantam Books.

Chang, Y. K., Tsai, C. L., & Chen, P. F. (2019). *Effects of acute and regular aerobic exercise on executive function across the lifespan: A systematic review.* Psychology & Health, 34(4), 415-437. DOI: [10 .1080/08870446.2018.1488832]

Chang Y. K., Tsai, C. L., & Chen, P. F. (2019). Effects of acute and regular aerobic exercise on executive function across the lifespan: A systematic review. Psychology & Health, 34(4), 415-437. DOI: 10.1080/08870446.2018.1488832

Chapman, G. (1995). *The 5 Love Languages: The Secret to Love That Lasts.* Northfield Publishing.

Firth, J., Stubbs, B., Vancampfort, D., et al. (2017). *Potential links between sedentary behaviour, mental health, and physical health.* BMC Medicine, 15, 23.

Gilbert, P. (2010). *Compassion Focused Therapy: Distinctive features.* Routledge.

Hirshkowitz, M., Whiton, K., Albert, S. M., et al. (2015*). National Sleep Foundation's sleep time duration recommendations: Methodology and results summary.* Sleep Health, 1(1), 40-43.

Jung, C. G. (1964). *Letters (Vol. 1).* Princeton University Press.

Jung, C. G. (1964). *Psychological Types (Vol. 6 of The Collected Works of C. G. Jung).* Princeton University Press.

Klein, M. (1991). *Envy and gratitude and other works 1946-1963.* Vintage.

Lee, D., Hannigan, B., & Murphy, R. (2018). *Vitamin D supplementation for depressive symptoms: A systematic review and meta-analysis.* Journal of Affective Disorders, 228, 17-26. DOI: [10.1016/j.jad.2017.12.009

Neff, K. D. (2003). *The Development and Validation of a Scale to Measure Self-Compassion.* Self and Identity, 2(3), 223–250.

Pontifex, M. B., Hillman, C. H., Castelli, D., & Kramer, A. F. (2009). *Aerobic fitness and cognitive control: Trade-offs between cognitive and cerebral processes.* Psychophysiology, 46(4), 845-852. DOI: [10.1111/j.1469-8986.2009.00807.x]

Porges, S. W. (2011). *The Polyvagal Theory: Neurophysiological Foundations of Emotions, Attachment, Communication, and Self-Regulation.* W.W. Norton & Company.

Pross, N., & Demnitz, N. (2010). *Dehydration: Physiology and consequences.* Progress in Brain Research, 193, 147-178.

Puetz, T. W., Patrick, K. E., & Dishman, R. K. (2008). *Effects of chronic exercise on feelings of energy and fatigue: A quantitative synthesis.* Psychology of Sport and Exercise, 9(3), 361-377. DOI: [10.1016/j.psychsport.2007.08.005]

Sherman, D. K., & Cohen, G. L. (2006). *The Self-Enhancement Motive.* In Handbook of Social Psychology (pp. 578-602). Sage Publications.

Smith, A., & Jones, B. (2020). *The effects of caffeine on anxiety and panic symptoms: A systematic review.* Journal of Anxiety Disorders, 66, 102–112.

www.ingramcontent.com/pod-product-compliance
Lightning Source LLC
Chambersburg PA
CBHW030923090426
42737CB00007B/301